212 POEMS THAT SAY

I love you

212 POEMS THAT SAY
I love you

Marcelle Clark

A BULL'S-EYE BOOK

Published by
William Mulvey Inc.
72 Park Street
New Canaan, Conn. 06840

Copyright © 1988 by William Mulvey Inc.
All rights reserved
including the right of reproduction
in whole or in part in any form.

Cover design: Clark Robinson
Interior design: Angela Foote

Library of Congress Cataloging-in-Publication Data

212 poems that say *I Love You*
"A Bull's-eye Book"

1. Love poetry. I. Clark, Marcelle. II. Title:
Two hundred twelve poems that say I love you.

PN6110.L6A15   1988   808.81'9354   88–42591

ISBN 0-934791-11-2

Printed in the United States of America
First Edition

*To all who are in Love,
have been in Love,
or hope to be in Love.*

Contents

∗∗∗

Marriage   1

Sonnet   *Christina Georgina Rossetti*   3
The Worn Wedding-Ring   *William C. Bennett*   4
Untitled   *Alice Cary*   7
My True-Love Hath My Heart   *Philip Sidney*   8
The Good-Morrow   *John Donne*   9
The Newly Wedded   *Winthrop Mackworth Praed*   10
A Match   *Algernon Charles Swinburne*   11
To Chloe   *William Cartwright*   13
Man and Wife   *Robert Lowell*   14
Marriage   *Babette Deutsch*   15
Dawn   *Frances Cornford*   16
Oh, No—Not Ev'n When First We Lov'd   *Thomas Moore*   17
A Song for My Mate   *Marguerite Wilkinson*   18
A Dedication to My Wife   *T. S. Eliot*   19
A Decade   *Amy Lowell*   20
Possession   *Bayard Taylor*   21
Marriage Morning   *Alfred, Lord Tennyson*   23
Sonnet XII   *Michael Drayton*   24
To Castara   *W. Habington*   25
A Song   *Robert Burns Wilson*   26
Love's Infiniteness   *John Donne*   27
A Wedding Song   *John Savary*   29
To Mrs. Bishop on the Anniversary of Her Wedding Day   *Samuel Bishop*   30
Proposal   *Bayard Taylor*   31

Love's Philosophy   *Percy Bysshe Shelley*   32
Sonnet LVII   *William Shakespeare*   33
The Heart of the Woman   *William Butler Yeats*   34
A Woman's Shortcomings   *Elizabeth Barrett Browning*   35
Songs Ascending   *Witter Bynner*   36
To One in Paradise   *Edgar Allan Poe*   37
Together   *Ludwig Lewisohn*   38
Amoret   *J. B. B. Nichols*   39
Surrender   *Amelia Josephine Burr*   41
When Death to Either Shall Come   *Robert Bridges*   42
The Marriage Ring   *George Crabbe*   43
In Those Old Days   *John Freeman*   44
The Reconciliation   *Alfred, Lord Tennyson*   45
Nearness   *John Freeman*   46

Love's Songs   47

Untitled   *Ben Jonson*   49
The First Day   *Christina Georgina Rossetti*   50
Untitled   *Edmund Spenser*   51
The Indian Serenade   *Anonymous*   52
I Love You, Dear   *George W. Crofts*   53
I Have Never Loved You Yet   *John Freeman*   54
Sonnet   *Elizabeth Barrett Browning*   55
Lovely Kind, and Kindly Loving   *Nicholas Breton*   56
Renouncement   *Alice Meynell*   57
Untitled   *Dinah Maria Muloch Craik*   58
In Deep Places   *Amelia Josephine Burr*   59
I Love Thee   *Thomas Hood*   60
How Many Times   *Thomas Lovell Beddoes*   61
Of Such As I Have   *Sarah Channing Woolsey*   62
Untitled   *Michael Drayton*   63
From Twelfth Night Act II Scene III   *William Shakespeare*   64
Since First I Saw Your Face   *Anonymous*   65
An Extravaganza   *Victor Hugo*   66

Untitled *William Shakespeare* 67
Love's Silence *Augusta Webster* 68
The Poet's Song to His Wife *B. W. Procter (Barry Cornwall)* 69
Four Words *Elizabeth Akers Allen* 70
Thornless Roses *Julia C. R. Dorr* 71
Love Me Not, Love, for that I First Loved Thee *Richard Watson Gilder* 72
Untitled *John Berryman* 73
The Lover Praises His Lady's Bright Beauty *Shaemas O'Sheel* 74
Calypso's Song to Ulysses *Adrian Mitchell* 75
Love Poem *Kathleen Raine* 76
Love Song *Harriet Monroe* 77
Believe Me, If All Those Endearing Young Charms *Thomas Moore* 78
The Sweetest Flower that Blows *Frederick Peterson* 79
Serenade at Noonday *Arthur Davison Ficke* 80
Strawberries *Edwin Morgan* 81
Corinna in Vendome *Pierre de Ronsard* 83
Song *Louise Bogan* 84
Love Song *Mary Carolyn Davies* 85
Before You Came *Marjorie Meeker* 86
Love Song *William Carlos Williams* 87
Love Pursued *Anonymous* 89
Thee, Thee, Only Thee *Thomas Moore* 90
A Song of a Young Lady to Her Ancient Lover *John Wilmot* 91
The Kiss *Thomas Moore* 92
The Sea-Shell *George MacDonald* 93
Happy Are They Who Kiss Thee *Aubrey De Vere* 94
Sudden Lights *Dante Gabriel Rossetti* 95
An Hour with Thee *Walter Scott* 96
The Passionate Shepherd to His Love *Christopher Marlowe* 97
Rondo *George Moore* 99
Entry April 28 *Walter Benton* 100
Untitled *Samuel Daniel* 101

From Indolence: XII   *Robert Bridges*   102
I'll Never Love Thee More   *James Graham*   103
Because   *Adelaide Anne Procter*   105
Psalm to My Beloved   *Eunice Tietjens*   107
Rest   *Irene Rutherford McLeod*   108
To His Mistress   *John Wilmot*   109
Untitled   *John Greenleaf Whittier*   110
The Lyric   *Percy Bysshe Shelley*   111
Beloved, My Beloved, When I Think   *Elizabeth Barrett Browning*   112
If Thou Must Love Me, Let It Be for Nought   *Elizabeth Barrett Browning*   113
Sonnet XLIII, from the Portuguese   *Elizabeth Barrett Browning*   114
Untitled   *Anonymous*   115
Sonnet   *Christina Georgina Rossetti*   117
Love   *Charles Swain*   118
Bedouin Song   *Bayard Taylor*   119
Constancy   *Joshua Sylvester*   121
How Many Times   *Thomas Lovell Beddoes*   122
Oblation   *Algernon Charles Swinburne*   123
Untitled   *Robert Louis Stevenson*   124
Sonnet   *Elizabeth Barrett Browning*   125
Song from a Drama   *Edmund Clarence Stedman*   126
Measure for Measure   *Harriet Prescott Spofford*   127
Forget Thee   *John Moultrie*   128
Untitled   *Alfred, Lord Tennyson*   129
Untitled   *Robert Burns*   130
Untitled   *Mathilde Blind*   131
Is It a Sin to Love Thee?   *Anonymous*   132
If You But Knew   *Anonymous*   135
Song   *Hermann Hagedorn*   136
In a Rose Garden   *John Bennett*   137
The Ladder   *Leonora Speyer*   139
A Woman's Last Word   *Robert Browning*   140
Serenade   *Henry Wadsworth Longfellow*   142
Untitled   *Sidney Godolphin*   143
She Walks in Beauty   *Lord Byron*   145

There Is None, O None but You   *Thomas Campion*   146
Ossian's Serenade   *Major Calder Campbell*   147
Alone in April   *James Branch Cabell*   148
Untitled   *Anonymous*   149
Nocturne   *Amelia Josephine Burr*   150
I Want You   *Arthur L. Gillom*   151
Now What Is Love   *Walter Raleigh*   153
Ah, How Sweet It Is to Love!   *John Dryden*   155
You Kissed Me   *Josephine Slocum Hunt*   156
Kissing   *Lord Herbert of Cherbury*   157
No and Yes   *Thomas Ashe*   158
Love's Philosophy   *Percy Bysshe Shelley*   159

Trust and Doubt   161

Young Love   *Theodosia Garrison*   163
Did Not   *Thomas Moore*   164
Untitled   *Anonymous*   165
Love Me at Last   *Alice Corbin*   166
Intimates   *D. H. Lawrence*   167
So Beautiful You Are Indeed   *Irene Rutherford McLeod*   168
Menace   *Katharine Tynan*   169
Untitled   *Matthew Arnold*   170
Untitled   *J. Fletcher*   171
Fullness of Love   *Elizabeth Barrett Browning*   172
Debts   *Jessie B. Rittenhouse*   173
Why So Pale and Wan   *John Suckling*   174
Do You Remember   *Thomas Haynes Bayly*   175
Kiss Me Softly   *John Godfrey Saxe*   176
Untitled   *William Shakespeare*   177
Untitled   *John Oldmixon*   178
Fidelis   *Adelaide Anne Procter*   179
Sweet Peril   *George MacDonald*   181
Serenade   *Richard Middleton*   182
Child, Child   *Sara Teasdale*   183
Untitled   *Attributed to Henry Hughes and Sir John Suckling*   184

Untitled   *Dante Gabriel Rossetti*   185
Song   *Christina Georgina Rossetti*   186
Love Not Me for Comely Grace   *Anonymous*   187
To a Lady Asking Him How Long He Would Love Her
   George Etherege   188

Separation   189

The Want of You   *Ivan Leonard Wright*   191
The Haunted Heart   *Jessie B. Rittenhouse*   192
When I Am Not with You   *Sara Teasdale*   193
Two Lips   *Thomas Hardy*   194
The Answering Voice   *Anna Hempstead Branch*   195
Bhartrhari   *Translated from the Sanskrit by John Brough*   196
Forgiven   *Helen Hunt Jackson*   197
Untitled   *e. e. cummings*   198
Postscript: For Gweno   *Alun Lewis*   199
Song: How Can I Care?   *Robert Graves*   200
Found   *Josephine Preston Peabody*   201
When We Are Parted   *Hamilton Aidé*   202
I Sought You   *John Hall Wheelock*   203
Parting   *Alice Freeman Palmer*   204
The Taxi   *Amy Lowell*   205
To Mary: I Sleep with Thee, and Wake with Thee
   John Clare   206
Untitled   *Anonymous*   207
A Song   *John Wilmot*   208
Gifts   *Juliana Horatia Ewing*   209
That Day You Came   *Lizette Woodworth Reese*   210
Untitled   *William Shakespeare*   211
Untitled   *Thomas Campion*   212
Telepathy   *James Russell Lowell*   213
Untitled   *Paul Verlaine*   214
At the Church Gate   *William M. Thackeray*   216
Untitled   *John Suckling*   218
The Wife to Her Husband   *Anonymous*   219
Apology   *Amy Lowell*   220

Untitled *John Suckling* 222
If Thou Wert By My Side *Reginald Heber* 223
To a Late Comer *Julia C. R. Dorr* 225
One *Arlo Bates* 226
Come to Me, Dearest *Joseph Brenan* 227
No One So Much As You *Edward Thomas* 229
Parting After a Quarrel *Eunice Tietjens* 231
Untitled *Walter Savage Landor* 232
Images *Richard Aldington* 233
You and I *Henry Alford* 234
The Lost Mistress *Robert Browning* 235
Untitled *Mathilde Blind* 236
Remember *Christina Georgina Rossetti* 237
Our Own *Margaret E. Sangster* 238
Song *Gerald Griffin* 239
Untitled *A. E. Housman* 240
Thou Hast Wounded the Spirit that Loved Thee *Mrs. David Porter* 241
I'll Remember You, Love, in My Prayers *Anonymous* 242
Night and Love *Edward George Earle Bulwer Lytton* 243
Star Song *Robert Underwood Johnson* 244
Miss You *David Cory* 245
Beloved, from the Hour that You Were Born *Corinne Roosevelt Robinson* 246
Farewell *John Addington Symonds* 247

Marriage
※

SONNET

O my heart's heart and you who are to me
More than myself myself, God be with you,
   Keep you in strong obedience, leal and true
To him whose noble service setteth free,
Give you all good we see or can foresee,
   Make your joys many and your sorrows few,
   Bless you in what you bear and what you do,
Yea, perfect you as He would have you be.
   So much for you; but what for me, dear friend?
   To love you without stint and all I can
To-day, to-morrow, world without an end:
   To love you much, and yet to love you more,
   As Jordan at its flood sweeps either shore;
Since woman is the helpmeet made for man.

                        Christina Georgina Rossetti

THE WORN WEDDING-RING
***

Your wedding-ring wears thin, dear wife; ah, summers not a few,
Since I put it on your finger first, have passed o'er me and you;
And, love, what changes we have seen,—what cares and pleasures, too,—
Since you became my own dear wife, when this old ring was new!

O, blessings on that happy day, the happiest of my life,
When, thanks to God. your low, sweet "Yes" made you my loving wife!
Your heart will say the same, I know; that day's as dear to you,—
That day that made me yours, dear wife, when this old ring was new.

How well do I remember now your young sweet face that day!
How fair you were, how dear you were, my tongue could hardly say;
Nor how I doated on you; Oh, how proud I was of you!
But did I love you more than now, when this old ring was new?

No—no! no fairer were you then than at this hour to me;
And, dear as life to me this day, how could you dearer be?
As sweet your face might be that day as now it is, 't is true;
But did I know your heart as well when this old ring was new?

O partner of my gladness, wife, what care, what grief is there
For me you would not bravely face, with me you would not share?

O, what a weary want had every day, if wanting you,
Wanting the love that God made mine when this old ring
  was new!

Years bring fresh links to bind us, wife,—young voices that
  are here;
Young faces round our fire that make their mother's yet more
  dear;
Young loving hearts your care each day makes yet more like
  to you,
More like the loving heart made mine when this old ring was
  new.

And blessed be God! all he has given are with us yet; around
Our table ever precious life lent to us still is found.
Though care we've known, with hopeful hearts the worst we've
  struggled through;
Blessed be his name for all his love since this old ring was
  new!

The past is dear, its sweetness still our memories treasure yet;
The griefs we've borne, together borne, we would not now
  forget.
Whatever, wife, the future brings, heart unto heart still true,
We'll share as we have shared all else since this old ring was
  new.

And if God spare us 'mongst our sons and daughters to grow
  old,
We know his goodness will not let your heart or mine grow
  cold.
Your aged eyes will see in mine all they've still shown to you,
And mine in yours all they have seen since this old ring was
  new.

And O, when death shall come at last to bid me to my rest,
May I die looking in those eyes, and resting on that breast;
O, may my parting gaze be blessed with the dear sight of
   you,
Of those fond eyes,—fond as they were when this old ring
   was new!

William C. Bennett

UNTITLED

Love's light is strange to you? Ah, me!
   Your heart is an unquickened seed,
And whatsoe'er your fortunes be,
   I tell you, you are poor indeed.

What toucheth it, it maketh bright,
   Yet loseth nothing, like the sun,
Within whose great and gracious light
   A thousand dew-drops shine as one.

Alice Cary

MY TRUE-LOVE HATH MY HEART

My true love hath my heart, and I have his,
By just exchange one for another given:
I hold his dear, and mine he cannot miss,
There never was a better bargain driven:
   My true-love hath my heart, and I have his.

His heart in me keeps him and me in one,
My heart in him his thoughts and senses guides:
He loves my heart, for once it was his own,
I cherish his because in me it bides:
   My true-love hath my heart, and I have his.

Philip Sidney

THE GOOD-MORROW

I wonder, by my troth, what thou and I
Did, till we lov'd? were we not wean'd till then?
But sucked on country pleasures, childishly?
Or snored we in the Seven Sleepers' den?
'Twas so; but this, all pleasures fancies be.
If ever any beauty I did see,
Which I desir'd, and got, 'twas but a dream of thee.

And now good morrow to our waking souls,
Which watch not one another out of fear;
For love all love of other sights controls,
And makes one little room an everywhere.
Let sea-discoverers to new worlds have gone;
Let maps to others, worlds on worlds have shown,
Let us possess one world: each hath one, and is one.

My face in thine eye, thine in mine appears,
And true plain hearts do in the faces rest:
Where can we find two better hemispheres,
Without sharp North, without declining West?
Whatever dies, was not mix'd equally;
If our two loves be one, or thou and I
Love so alike that none do slacken, none can die.

John Donne

THE NEWLY WEDDED

Now the rite is duly done,
  Now the word is spoken,
And the spell has made us one
  Which may ne'er be broken:
Rest we, dearest, in our home,—
  Roam we o'er the heather,—
We shall rest, and we shall roam,
  Shall we not? together.

From this hour the summer rose
  Sweeter breathes to charm us;
From this hour the winter snows
  Lighter fall to harm us:
Fair or foul—on land or sea—
  Come the wind or weather,
Best or worst, whate'er they be,
  We shall share together.

Death, who friend from friend can part,
  Brother rend from brother,
Shall but link us, heart and heart,
  Closer to each other:
We will call his anger play,
  Deem his dart a feather,
When we meet him on our way
  Hand in hand together.

Winthrop Mackworth Praed

A MATCH

If love were what the rose is,
    And I were like the leaf,
Our lives would grow together
In sad or singing weather,
Blown fields or flowerful closes,
    Green pleasure or gray grief;
If love were what the rose is,
    And I were like the leaf.

If I were what the words are,
    And love were like the tune,
With double sound and single
Delight our lips would mingle,
With kisses glad as birds are
    That get sweet rain at noon;
If I were what the words are,
    And love were like the tune.

If you were life, my darling,
    And I your love were death,
We'd shine and snow together
Ere March made sweet the weather
With daffodil and starling
    And hours of fruitful breath;
If you were life, my darling,
    And I your love were death.

If you were thrall to sorrow,
    And I were page to joy,
We'd play for lives and seasons
With loving looks and treasons
And tears of night and morrow
    And laughs of maid and boy;

If you were thrall to sorrow,
   And I were page to joy.

If you were April's lady,
   And I were lord in May,
We'd throw with leaves for hours
And draw for days with flowers,
Till day like night were shady
   And night were bright like day;
If you were April's lady,
   And I were lord in May.

If you were queen of pleasure,
   And I were king of pain,
We'd hunt down love together,
Pluck out his flying-feather,
And teach his feet a measure,
   And find his mouth a rein;
If you were queen of pleasure,
   And I were king of pain.

            Algernon Charles Swinburne

TO CHLOE
Who for His Sake Wished Herself Younger

There are two births; the one when light
   First strikes the new awaken'd sense;
The other when two souls unite,
   And we must count our life from thence:
When you loved me and I loved you
The both of us were born anew.

Love then to us new souls did give
   And in those souls did plant new powers;
Since when another life we live,
   The breath we breathe is his, not ours:
Love makes those young whom age doth chill,
And whom he finds young keeps young still.

William Cartwright

MAN AND WIFE

Tamed by *Miltown*, we lie on Mother's bed;
the rising sun in war paint dyes us red;
in broad daylight her gilded bed-posts shine,
abandoned, almost Dionysian.
At last the trees are green on Marlborough Street,
blossoms on our magnolia ignite
the morning with their murderous five days' white.
All night I've held your hand,
as if you had
a fourth time faced the kingdom of the mad—
its hackneyed speech, its homicidal eye—
and dragged me home alive . . . Oh my *Petite*,
clearest of all God's creatures, still all air and nerve:
you were in your twenties, and I,
once hand on glass
and heart in mouth,
outdrank the Rahvs in the heat
of Greenwich Village, fainting at your feet—
too boiled and shy
and poker-faced to make a pass,
while the shrill verve
of your invective scorched the traditional South.

Now twelve years later, you turn your back.
Sleepless, you hold
your pillow to your hollows like a child,
your old-fashioned tirade—
loving, rapid, merciless—
breaks like the Atlantic Ocean on my head.

Robert Lowell

MARRIAGE

Not any more, not ever while I live
With you, shall I be single or be whole.
A wife is one who cannot cease to give
Flowers of her body, and graftings from her soul.

I came to bud for you like a young tree;
And though I should not give you any fruit,
here is one orchard where your hands make free.
Something is always tugging at my root.

Though you abandon what you once found sweet,
I shall be like a birch whose bark is torn
By fingers scratching difficult, incomplete
Confessions of an outlived love and scorn.

And though I wither near you, patiently
As any bough that any wind can break,
You will go on having as much of me
As winter from a stricken limb can take.

You are my winter, as you are my spring.
However we pretend, this will be true.
You are the wind that makes the leafage sing
And strips the branches that it quivers through.

Babette Deutsch

DAWN

So begins the day,
Solid, chill, and gray,
But my heart will wake
Happy for your sake;
No more tossed and wild,
Singing like a child,
Quiet as a flower
In this first gray hour.

So my heart will wake
Happy, for your sake.

Frances Cornford

OH, NO—NOT EV'N WHEN FIRST WE LOV'D

Oh, no—not ev'n when first we lov'd
   Wert thou as dear as now thou art;
Thy beauty then my senses move'd,
   But now thy virtues bind my heart.
What was but Passion's sigh before
   Has since been turn'd to Reason's vow;
And, though I then might love thee *more*,
   Trust me, I love thee *better* now.

Although my heart in earlier youth
   Might kindle with more wild desire,
Believe me, it has gain'd in truth
   Much more than it has lost in fire.
The flame now warms my inmost core
   That then but sparkled o'er my brow,
And though I seem'd to love thee more,
   Yet, oh, I love thee better now.

Thomas Moore

A SONG FOR MY MATE

Higher than the slim eucalyptus,
Higher than the dim, purple mountains,
Higher than the stern flight of eagles,
   Rose our young hopes, long, long ago.

Sweeter than wild, sweet berries,
Sweeter than a chill spring's bounty,
Sweeter than a meadowlark's carol,
   Were the young, sweet joys that we shared.

More bitter than a swelling olive,
More bitter than brackish river,
More bitter than a crow's hard laughter,
   Were the sorrows we have known, my dear.

But nearer than the light is to the day,
And nearer than the night is to darkness,
And nearer than the winds to their crooning,
   I am drawn, I am held to your heart.

Marguerite Wilkinson

A DEDICATION TO MY WIFE

To whom I owe the leaping delight
That quickens my sense in our wakingtime
And the rhythm that governs the repose of our sleepingtime,
  The breathing in unison

Of lovers whose bodies smell of each other
Who think the same thoughts without need of speech
And babble the same speech without need of meaning.
No peevish winter wind shall chill
No sullen tropic sun shall wither
The roses in the rose-garden which is ours and ours only

But this dedication is for others to read:
These are private words addressed to you in public.

T. S. Eliot

A DECADE

When you came, you were like red wine and honey,
And the taste of you burnt my mouth with its sweetness.
Now you are like morning bread,
I hardly taste you at all for I know your savor,
But I am completely nourished.

Amy Lowell

POSSESSION
***

"It was our wedding-day
A month ago," dear heart, I hear you say.
If months, or years, or ages since have passed,
I know not: I have ceased to question Time.
I only know that once there pealed a chime
Of joyous bells, and then I held you fast,
And all stood back, and none my right denied,
And forth we walked: the world was free and wide
Before us. Since that day
I count my life: the Past is washed away.

It was no dream, that vow:
It was the voice that woke me from a dream,—
A happy dream, I think; but I am waking now,
And drink the splendor of a sun supreme
That turns the mist of former tears to gold.
Within these arms I hold
The fleeting promise, chased so long in vain:
Ah, weary bird! thou wilt not fly again:
Thy wings are clipped, thou canst no more depart,—
Thy nest is builded in my heart!

I was the crescent, thou
The silver phantom of the perfect sphere
Held in its bosom: in one glory now
Our lives united shine, and many a year—
Not the sweet moon of bridal only—we
One lustre, ever at the full, shall be:
One pure and rounded light, one planet whole,
One life developed, one completed soul!
For I in thee, and thou in me,
United our cloven halves of destiny.

God knew his chosen time:
He bade me slowly ripen to my prime,

And from my boughs withheld the promised fruit,
Till storm and sun gave vigor to the root.
Secure, O Love! secure
Thy blessing is: I have thee day and night:
Thou art become my blood, my life, my light:
God's mercy thou, and therefore shalt endure.

Bayard Taylor

MARRIAGE MORNING

Light, so low upon earth,
   You send a flash to the sun.
Here is the golden close of love,
   All my wooing is done.
Oh, the woods and the meadows,
   Woods where we hid from the wet,
Stiles where we stay'd to be kind,
   Meadows in which we met!

Light, so low in the vale
   You flash and lighten afar,
For this is the golden morning of love,
   And you are his morning star.
Flash, I am coming, I come,
   By meadow and stile and wood,
Oh, lighten into my eyes and heart,
   Into my heart and my blood!

Heart, are you great enough
   For a love that never tires?
O heart, are you great enough for love?
   I have heard of thorns and briers.
Over the thorns and briers,
   Over the meadows and stiles,
Over the world to the end of it
   Flash for a million miles.

Alfred, Lord Tennyson

SONNET XII

You're not alone when you are still alone;
O God, from you that I could private be!
Since you one were, I never since was one,
Since you in me, my self since out of me,
Transported from my self into your being,
Though either distant, present yet to either;
Senseless with too much joy, each other seeing,
And only absent when we are together.
Give me my self, and take your self again!
Devise some means but how I may forsake you!
So much is mine that doth with you remain,
That taking what is mine, with me I take you.
   You do bewitch me! O that I could fly
   From my self you, or from your own self I!

Michael Drayton

TO CASTARA
**

We saw and woo'd each other's eyes,
   My soul contracted then with thine,
And both burnt in one sacrifice,
   By which our marriage grew divine.

Let wilder youths, whose soul is sense,
   Profane the temple of delight,
And purchase endless penitence,
   With the stol'n pleasure of one night.

Time's ever ours, while we despise
   The sensual idol of our clay,
For though the sun do set and rise,
   We joy one everlasting day.

Whose light no jealous clouds obscure,
   While each of us shine innocent,
The troubled stream is still impure;
   With virtue flies away content.

And though opinions often err,
   We'll court the modest smile of fame,
For sin's black danger circles her,
   Who hath infection in her name.

Thus when to one dark silent room
   Death shall our loving coffins thrust:
Fame will build columns on our tomb,
   And add a perfume to our dust.

W. Habington

A SONG

I do not ask—dear love—not I,
  A jewelled crown to win,
Nor robe, nor crown—nor do I cry
To those that guard the gates of heaven,
  That they should let me in.

Oh, when they talk of far-off strands,
  I have no heart to pray,
So lonely seem those heavenly lands,
I feel no wish for angel hands
  To wipe my tears away.

I care not for the joyous throng,
  My soul could never share
The endless bliss—the happy song;
How long the days, O God, how long,
  If I should miss thee there!

Nay, love; I only could be blest
  Close by thy side to be,
To hold thy hand—to lean at rest,
Forever on thy faithful breast,
  That would be heaven for me.

Robert Burns Wilson

LOVE'S INFINITENESS

If yet I have not all thy love,
   Dear, I shall never have it all,
I cannot breathe one other sigh, to move,
   Nor can entreat one other tear to fall.
And all my treasure, which should purchase thee,
   Sighs, tears, and oaths, and letters I have spent,
Yet no more can be due to me
   Than at the bargain made was meant:
If then thy gift of love were partial,
That some to me, some should to others fall,
Dear, I shall never have thee all.

Or if then thou gavest me all,
   All was but all, which thou hadst then;
But if in thy heart, since, there be or shall
   New love created be, by other men,
Which have their stocks entire, and can in tears,
   In sighs, in oaths, and letters outbid me,
This new love may beget new fears,
   For this love was not vowed by thee.
And yet it was, thy gift being general,
The ground, thy heart is mine, whatever shall
Grow there, dear, I should have it all.

Yet I would not have all yet;
   He that hath all can have no more;
And since my love doth every day admit
   New growth, thou shouldst have new rewards in store:
Thou canst not every day give me thy heart;
   If thou canst give it, then thou never gavest it.

Love's riddles are that though thy heart depart
    It stays at home, and thou, with losing, savest it:
But we will have a way more liberal
Than changing hearts—to join them; so we shall
Be one, and one another's all.

John Donne

A WEDDING SONG

Two roses growing on a single tree,
Two faces bending o'er a silver spring,
Two pairs of eyes that their own image see,
And set the heavens within a little ring,
Two children in this naughty world of ours,
      Linked by the marriage powers.

Undo the things from off your feet,—
This spot at least is holy ground.
The solitude is wild and sweet,
Where no base thing is found.
There watch, or wander in that Paradise
      Till soft moon-rise.

Sink through the soundless world of dreams,
Or climb the secret stairs of bliss,
And tiptoe stand where brightest gleams
The heaven of heavens within a kiss;
Sleep through the soft hours of rosy morn;
      Urania, be born!

Sleep while the moist star trembles in the dews,
And when in sunrise gleams the lake of glass;
Sleep while the heavens are interchanging hues,
And Saturn's tear "rolls down the blade of glass;"
Wake when the birds are singing in the trees,
      And sing like these.

John Savary

TO MRS. BISHOP ON THE ANNIVERSARY OF HER WEDDING DAY

'Thee, Mary, with this ring I wed,'
So, fourteen years ago, I said—
Behold, another ring!—'For what?'
'To wed thee o'er again—why not?'
With that first ring I married Youth
Grace, Beauty, Innocence, and Truth;
Taste long admired, since long revered,
And all my Molly then appeared.
If she, by merit since disclosed,
Prove twice the woman I supposed,
I plead that double merit now,
To justify a double vow.
Here then, today (with faith as sure,
With ardour as intense, as pure,
As when, amidst the rites divine,
I took thy troth, and plighted mine),
To thee, sweet girl, my second ring
A token, and a pledge, I bring;
With this I wed, till death us part,
Thy riper virtues to my heart;
Those virtues, which, before untried,
The wife had added to the bride;
Those virtues, whose progressive claim
Endearing wedlock's very name,
My soul enjoys, my song approves,
For Conscience's sake, as well as Love's.
And why?—They show me every hour,
Honour's high thought, affection's power,
Discretion's deed, sound Judgement's sentence,
And teach me all things—but Repentance.

Samuel Bishop

PROPOSAL
***

The violet loves a sunny bank,
    The cowslip loves the lea,
The scarlet creeper loves the elm;
    But I love—thee.

The sunshine kisses mount and vale,
    The stars, they kiss the sea,
The west winds kiss the clover bloom,
    But I kiss—thee.

The oriole weds his mottled mate,
    The lily's bride o' the bee;
Heaven's marriage ring is round the earth—
    Shall I wed thee?

Bayard Taylor

LOVE'S PHILOSOPHY

The fountains mingle with the river
   And the rivers with the ocean,
The winds of heaven mix for ever
   With a sweet emotion;
Nothing in the world is single,
   All things by a law divine
In one another's being mingle—
   Why not I with thine?

See the mountains kiss high heaven,
   And the waves clasp one another;
No sister-flower would be forgiven
   If it disdained its brother:
And the sunlight clasps the earth,
   And the moonbeams kiss the sea—
What are all these kissings worth,
   If thou kiss not me?

Percy Bysshe Shelley

SONNET LVII
*

Being your slave, what should I do but tend
Upon the hours and times of your desire?
I have no precious time at all to spend,
Nor services to do, till you require.
Nor dare I chide the world-without-end hour
Whilst I, my sovereign, watch the clock for you,
Nor think the bitterness of absence sour
When you have bid your servant once adieu;
Nor dare I question with my jealous thought
Where you may be, or your affairs suppose,
But, like a sad slave, stay and think of nought
Save, where you are how happy you make those.
   So true a fool is love that in your will,
   Though you do anything, he thinks no ill.

William Shakespeare

THE HEART OF THE WOMAN

O what to me the little room
That was brimmed up with prayer and rest;
He bade me out into the gloom
And my breast lies on his breast.

O what to me my mother's care,
The house where I was safe and warm;
The shadowy blossom of my hair
Will hide us from the bitter storm.

O hiding hair and dewy eyes,
I am no more with life or death,
My heart upon his warm heart lies,
My breath is mixed into his breath.

William Butler Yeats

A WOMAN'S SHORTCOMINGS

Unless you can think, when the song is done,
   No other is soft in the rhythm;
Unless you can feel, when left by one,
   That all men else go with him;
Unless you can know, when unpraised by his breath,
   That your beauty itself wants proving;
Unless you can swear, "For life, for death!"—
   Oh fear to call it loving!

Unless you can muse in a crowd all day,
   On the absent face that fixed you;
Unless you love, as the angels may,
   With the breadth of heaven betwixt you;
Unless you can dream that his fast is fast,
   Through behoving and unbehoving;
Unless you can die when the dream is past—
   Oh never call it loving!

Elizabeth Barrett Browning

SONGS ASCENDING

Love has been sung a thousand ways—
　So let it be;
The songs ascending in your praise
Through all my days
　Are three.

Your cloud-white body first I sing;
　Your love was heaven's blue,
And I, a bird, flew carolling
In ring on ring
　Of you.

Your nearness is the second song;
　When God began to be,
And bound you strongly, right or wrong,
With his own thong,
　To me.

But oh, the song, eternal, high,
　That tops these two!—
You live forever, you who die,
I am not I
　But you.

　　　　　　　　Witter Bynner

TO ONE IN PARADISE

Thou wast all that to me, love,
   For which my soul did pine—
A green isle in the sea, love,
   A fountain and a shrine,
All wreathed with fairy fruits and flowers,
   And all the flowers were mine.

Ah, dream too bright to last!
   Ah, starry Hope! that didst arise
But to be overcast!
   A voice from out the Future cries,
'On! On!'—but o'er the Past
   (Dim gulf!) my spirit hovering lies
Mute, motionless, aghast!

For, alas! alas! with me
   The light of life is o'er!
No more—no more—no more—
(Such language holds the solemn sea
   To the sands upon the shore)
Shall bloom the thunder-blasted tree
   Or the stricken eagle soar!

And all my days are trances
   And all my nightly dreams
Are where thy grey eye glances,
   And where thy footsteps gleams—
In what eternal dances,
   By what eternal streams.

Edgar Allan Poe

TOGETHER
*
* *

You and I by this lamp with these
Few books shut out the world. Our knees
Touch almost in this little space.
But I am glad. I see your face.
The silences are long, but each
Hears the other without speech.
And in this simple scene there is
The essence of all subtleties,
The freedom from all fret and smart,
The one sure sabbath of the heart.

The world—we cannot conquer it,
Nor change the mind of fools one whit.
Here, here alone do we create
Beauty and peace inviolate;
Here night by night and hour by hour
We build a high impregnable tower
Whence may shine, now and again,
A light to light the feet of men
When they see the rays thereof:
And this is marriage, this is love.

Ludwig Lewisohn

AMORET
***

Love found you still a child,
Who looked on him and smiled
Scornful with laughter mild
   And knew him not:

Love turned and looked on you,
Love looked and he smiled too,
And all at once you knew
   You knew not what.

Love laughed again, and said
Smiling, "Be not afraid:
Though lord of all things made,
   I do no wrong:
Like you I love all flowers,
All dusky twilight hours,
Spring sunshine and Spring showers,
   Like you am young."

Love looked into your eyes,
Your clear cold idle eyes,
Said, "These shall be my prize,
   Their light my light;
These tender lips that move
With laughter soft as love
Shall tremble still and prove
   Love's very might."

Love took you by the hand
At eve, and bade you stand
At edge of the woodland,
   Where I should pass;
Love sent me thither, sweet,
And brought me to your feet;
He willed that we should meet,
   And so it was.

                        J.B.B. Nichols

SURRENDER

As I look back upon your first embrace
I understand why from your sudden touch
Angered I sprang, and struck you in the face.
You asked at once too little and too much.
But now that of my spirit you require
Love's very soul that unto death endures,
Crown as you will the cup of your desire—
   I am all yours.

Amelia Josephine Burr

WHEN DEATH TO EITHER SHALL COME

When Death to either shall come,—
   I pray it be first to me,—
Be happy as ever at home,
   If so, as I wish, it be.

Possess thy heart, my own;
   And sing to thy child on thy knee,
Or read to thyself alone
   The songs that I made for thee.

Robert Bridges

THE MARRIAGE RING
***

The ring, so worn as you behold,
So thin, so pale, is yet of gold:
The passion such it was to prove—
Worn with life's care, love yet was love.

George Crabbe

IN THOSE OLD DAYS

*
**

In those old days you were called beautiful,
But I have worn the beauty from your face;
The flowerlike bloom has withered on your cheek
With the harsh years, and the fire in your eyes
Burns darker now and deeper, feeding on
Beauty and the rememberance of things gone.
Even your voice is altered when you speak,
Or is grown mute with old anxiety
      For me.

Even as fire leaps into flame and burns
Leaping and laughing in its lovely flight
And then under the flame a glowing dome
Deepens slowly into blood-like light:—
So did you flame and in flame take delight,
So are you hollow'd now with aching fire.
But I still warm me and make there my home,
Still beauty and youth burn there invisibly
      For me

Now my lips falling on your silver'd skull,
My fingers in the valleys of your cheeks,
Or my hands in your thin strong hands fast caught,
Your body clutched to mine, mine bent to yours:
Now love indying feeds on love beautiful,
Now, now I am but thought kissing your thought.
—And can it be in your heart's music speaks
A deeper rhythm hearing mine: can it be
      Indeed for me.

John Freeman

THE RECONCILIATION

As through the land at eve we went,
   And plucked the ripened ears,
We fell out, my wife and I,
   And kissed again with tears.

And blessings on the falling out
   That all the more endears,
When we fall out with those we love
   And kiss again with tears.

For when we came where lies the child
   We lost in other years,
There above the little grave,
O, there above the little grave,
   We kissed again with tears.

Alfred, Lord Tennyson

NEARNESS

Thy hand my hand,
Thine eyes my eyes,
All of thee
Caught and confused with me:
My hand thy hand,
My eyes thine eyes,
All of me
Sunken and discovered anew in thee . . .

No: still
A foreign mind,
A thought
By other yet uncaught;
A secret will
Strange as the wind:
The heart of thee
Bewildering with strange fire the heart in me.

Hand touches hand,
Eye to eye beckons,
But who shall guess
Another's loneliness?
Though hand grasp hand,
Though the eye quickens,
Still lone as night
Remain thy spirit and mine, past touch and sight.

John Freeman

Love's Songs

UNTITLED

Drink to me only with thine eyes,
   And I will pledge with mine;
Or leave a kiss but in the cup
   And I'll not look for wine.
The thirst that from the soul doth rise
   Doth ask a drink divine;
But might I of Jove's nectar sup,
   I would not change for thine.

I sent thee late a rosy wreath,
   Not so much honouring thee
As giving it a hope that there
   I could not withered be;
But thou thereon didst only breathe
   And sent'st it back to me;
Since when it grows, and smells, I swear,
   Not of itself, but thee.

Ben Jonson

THE FIRST DAY

I wish I could remember the first day,
First hour, first moment of your meeting me;
If bright or dim the season, it might be
Summer or winter for aught I can say.
So unrecorded did it slip away,
So blind was I to see and to foresee,
So dull to mark the budding of my tree
That would not blossom yet for many a May.
If only I could recollect it! Such
A day of days! I let it come and go
As traceless as a thaw of by gone snow.
It seemed to mean so little, meant so much!
If only now I could recall that touch,
First touch of hand in hand!—Did one but know!

Christina Georgina Rossetti

UNTITLED
***

One day I wrote her name upon the strand,
   But came the waves and washèd it away:
Again I wrote it with a second hand,
   But came the tide, and made my pains his prey.
'Vain man,' said she, 'thou do'st in vain assay,
   A mortal thing so to immortalize,
For I myself shall like to this decay,
   And eek my name be wipèd out likewise.'
'Not so,' quoth I, 'let baser things devise
   To die in dust, but you shall live by fame:
My verse your virtues rare shall eternize,
   And in the heavens write your glorious name,
     Where, whenas death shall all the world subdue,
     Our love shall live, and later life renew.'

Edmund Spenser

THE INDIAN SERENADE

I arise from dreams of thee
In the first sweet sleep of night,
When the winds are breathing low,
And the stars are shining bright:
I arise from dreams of thee,
And a spirit in my feet
Hath led me—who knows how?
To thy chamber window, Sweet!

Anonymous

I LOVE YOU, DEAR
*
**

"I love you, dear!" and saying this,
   My heart responds, " 'T is true! it is true!"
And thrills with more than earthly bliss
   While still I say, "I love but you!"

"Why should I love you, dear?" you ask,
   As though true love could reason why;
If love could think, it would be a task
   For me to love, and love would die.

I love you just because I do.
   The key I do not care to find,
For fear the strands would break in two
   That me a willing captive bind.

The fact is all I want to know,
   I will not grieve while that is given;
To lose my love would be my woe;
   To keep it as it is, is heaven.

George W. Crofts

I HAVE NEVER LOVED YOU YET

I have never loved you yet, if now I love.

If Love was born in that bright April sky
And ran unheeding when the sun was high,
And slept as the moon sleeps through Autumn nights
While those clear steady stars burn in their heights:

If Love so lived and ran and slept and woke
And ran in beauty when each morning broke,
Love yet was boylike, fervid and unstable,
Teased with romance, not knowing truth from fable.

But Winter after Autumn comes and stills
The petulant waters and the wild mind fills
With silence; and the dark and cold are bitter,
O, bitter to remember past days sweeter.

Then Spring with one warm cloudy finger breaks
The frost and the heart's airless black soil shakes;
Love grown a man uprises, serious, bright
With mind remembering now things dark and light.

O, if young Love was beautiful, Love grown old,
Experienced and grave is not grown cold.
Life's faithful fire in Love's heart burns the clearer
With all that was, is and draws darkling nearer.

I have never loved you yet, if now I love.

John Freeman

SONNET

When two souls stand up erect and strong,
Face to face, silent, drawing night and nigher,
Until the lengthening wings break into fire
At either curvèd point,—what bitter wrong
Can the earth do us, that we should not long
Be here contented? Think. In mounting higher,
The angels would press on us and aspire
To drop some golden orb of perfect song
Into our deep, dear silence. Let us stay
Rather on earth, Belovèd,—where the unfit
Contrarious moods of men recoil away
And isolate pure spirits, and permit
A place to stand and love in for a day,
With darkness and the death-hour rounding it.

Elizabeth Barrett Browning

LOVELY KIND, AND KINDLY LOVING

Lovely kind, and kindly loving,
Such a mind were worth the moving:
Truly fair, and fairly true,
Where are all these, but in you?

Wisely kind, and kindly wise,
Blessèd life, where such love lies!
Wise, and kind, and fair, and true,
Lovely live all these in you.

Sweetly dear, and dearly sweet,
Blessèd where these blessings meet!
Sweet, fair, wise, kind, blessèd, true,
Blessèd be all these in you!

Nicholas Breton

RENOUNCEMENT

I must not think of thee; and, tired yet strong,
I shun the thought that lurks in all delight—
The thought of thee—and in the blue heaven's height,
And in the dearest passage of a song.
Oh, just beyond the fairest thoughts that throng
This breast, the thought of thee waits, hidden yet bright
But it must never, never come in sight;
I must stop short of thee the whole day long.
But when sleep comes to close each difficult day,
When night gives pause to the long watch I keep,
And all my bonds I needs must loose apart,
Must doff my will as raiment laid away,—
With the first dream that comes with the first sleep
I run, I run, I am gathered to thy heart.

Alice Meynell

UNTITLED

***

I love you. Words are small;
'T is life speaks plain: In twenty years
Perhaps you may know all.

Dinah Maria Muloch Craik

IN DEEP PLACES

I love thee, dear, and knowing mine own heart
With every beat I give God thanks for this;
I love thee only for the self thou art;
No wild embrace, no wisdom-shaking kiss,
No passionate pleading of a heart laid bare,
No urgent cry of love's extremity—
Strong traps to take the spirit unaware—
Not one of these I ever had of thee.
Neither of passion nor of pity wrought
Is this, the love to which at last I yield,
But shapen in the stillness of my thought
And by a birth of agony revealed.
Here is a thing to live while we do live
Which honors thee to take and me to give.

Amelia Josephine Burr

I LOVE THEE

I love thee—I love thee!
'T is all that I can say;
It is my vision in the night,
   My dreaming in the day;
The very echo of my heart,
   The blessing when I pray.
I love thee—I love thee!

I love thee—I love thee!
   Is ever on my tongue.
In all my proudest poesy
   That chorus still is sung;
It is the verdict of my eyes
   Amidst the gay and young:
I love thee—I love thee!
   A thousand maids among.

I love thee—I love thee!
   Thy bright and hazel glance,
The mellow lute upon those lips,
   Whose tender tones entrance.
But most dear heart of hearts, thy proofs.
   That still these words enhance!
I love thee—I love thee!
   Whatever be thy chance.

Thomas Hood

HOW MANY TIMES
*
**

How many times do I love thee, dear?
   Tell me how many thoughts there be
      In the atmosphere
      Of a new-fallen year,
Whose white and sable hours appear
   The latest flake of Eternity:
So many things do I love thee, dear.

How many times do I love, again?
   Tell me how many beads there are
      In a silver chain
      Of the evening rain,
Unravelled from the tumbling main,
   And threading the eye of a yellow star:
So many times do I love, again.

Thomas Lovell Beddoes

OF SUCH AS I HAVE

Love me for what I am, Love. Not for sake
Of some imagined thing which I might be,
Some brightness or some goodness not in me,
Born of your hope, as dawn to eyes that wake
Imagined morns before the morning break.
If I, to please you (whom I fain would please),
Reset myself like new key to old tune,
Chained thought, remodelled action, very soon
My hand would slip from yours, and by degrees
The loving, faulty friend, so close to-day,
Would vanish, and another take her place,—
A stranger with a stranger's scrutinies,
A new regard, an unfamiliar face.
Love me for what I am, then, if you may;
But if you cannot,—love me either way.

Sarah Channing Woolsey

UNTITLED
***

So well I love thee, as without thee I
Love nothing; if I might choose, I'd rather die
That be one day debarr'd thy company.

Since beasts, and plants do grow, and live and move,
Beasts are those men, that such a life approve:
He only lives, that deadly is in love.

The corn that in the ground is sown first dies
And of one seed do many ears arise:
Love, this world's corn, by dying multiplies.

The seeds of love first by thy eyes were thrown
Into a ground untill'd, a heart unknown
To bear such fruit, till by thy hands 'twas sown.

Look as your looking-glass by chance may fall,
Divide and break in many pieces small
And yet shows forth the selfsame face in all:

Proportions, features, graces just the same,
And in the smallest piece as well the name
Of fairest one deserves, as in the richest frame.

So all my thoughts are pieces but of you
Which put together makes a glass so true
As I therein no other's face but yours can view.

Michael Drayton

From TWELFTH NIGHT *Act II, Scene iii*
***

O mistress mine, where are you roaming?
O, stay and hear; your true-love's coming,
   That can sing both high and low:
Trip no further, pretty sweeting;
Journeys end in lovers' meeting,
   Every wise man's son doth know.

What is love? 'tis not hereafter;
Present mirth hath present laughter;
   What's to come is still unsure:
In delay there lies no plenty;
Then come kiss me, sweet-and-twenty,
   Youth's a stuff will not endure.

William Shakespeare

SINCE FIRST I SAW YOUR FACE

Since first I saw your face I resolved to honour and reknown ye;
If now I am disdainèd I wish my heart had never known ye.
What? I that loved and you that liked, shall we begin to wrangle?
No, no, no, my heart is fast, and cannot disentangle.
If I admire or praise you too much, that fault you may forgive me;
Or if my hands had stray'd but a touch, then justly might you leave me.
I ask'd you leave, you bade me love; is't now a time to chide me?
No, no, no, I'll love you still what fortune e'er betide me.
The Sun, whose beams most glorious are, rejecteth no beholder,
And your sweet beauty past compare made my poor eyes the bolder:
Where beauty moves and wit delights and signs of kindness bind me,
There, O there, whe'er I go I'll leave my heart behind me!

Anonymous

AN EXTRAVAGANZA
*
* *

I'd give, Girl (were I but a king),
Throne, sceptre, empire,—everything:
My people suppliant on the knee;
My ships that crowd the subject sea;
My crown, my baths of porphyry,
   For *one* sweet look from thee!

Were I a god, I'd give—the air,
Earth, and the sea; the angels fair;
The skies; the golden worlds around;
The demons whom my laws have bound;
Chaos and its dark progeny;
All space and all eternity,
   For *one* love-kiss from thee!

Victor Hugo

UNTITLED
***

Shall I compare thee to a summer's day?
    Thou art more lovely and more temperate:
Rough winds do shake the darling buds of May,
    And summer's lease hath all too short a date:
Sometimes too hot the eye of heaven shines,
    And often is his gold complexion dimmed;
And every fair from fair sometimes declines,
    By chance, or nature's changing course untrimmed;
But thy eternal summer shall not fade,
    Nor lose possession of that fair thou owest,
Nor shall death brag thou wanderest in his shade,
    When in eternal lines to time thou growest;
      So long as men can breathe, or eyes can see,
    So long lives this, and this gives life to thee.

William Shakespeare

LOVE'S SILENCE

Dearest, this one day our own,
   Stolen from the crowd and press,
We two, heart to heart, alone;
   Any speech were less.

We are weary, even thus,
   Talk might turn to discontent,
   Else be practised merriment;
Earth and sky will speak for us
   Nearer as we meant.

We two, in the stillness, dear,
   Fair dreams come without our quest,
   Not to speak of life is best.
Ah, our holiday is here,
   Let it all be rest.

Augusta Webster

THE POET'S SONG TO HIS WIFE

How many summers, love,
   Have I been thine?
How many days, thou dove,
   Hast thou been mine?
Time, like the wingèd wind
   When 't bends the flowers,
Hath left no mark behind
   To count the hours!

Some weight of thought, though loth,
   On thee he leaves;
Some lines of care round both
   Perhaps he weaves:
Some fears,—a soft regret
   For joys scarce known:
Sweet looks we half forget;—
   All else is flown!

Ah!—With what thankless heart
   I mourn and sing!
Look where our children start,
   Like sudden spring!
With tongues all sweet and low,
   Like a pleasant rhyme,
They tell how much I owe
   To thee and time!

      B. W. Procter (Barry Cornwall)

FOUR WORDS

Beloved, the briefest words are best;
   And all the fine euphonious ways
In which the truth has been expressed
     Since Adam's early Eden days,
       Could never match the simple phrase,—
         Sweetheart, I love you!

If I should say the world were blank
   Without your face; if I should call
The stars to witness, rank on rank,
     That I am true although they fall,—
       'T would mean but this,—and this means all,—
         Sweetheart, I love you!

And so, whatever change is wrought
   By time or fate, delight or dole,
One single, happy, helpful thought
     Makes strong and calm my steady soul,
       And these sweet words contain the whole,—
         Sweetheart, I love you!

I will not wrong their truth to-day
   By wild, impassioned vows of faith,
Since all that volumes could convey
     Is compassed thus in half a breath,
       Which holds and hallows life and death,—
         Sweetheart, I love you!

Elizabeth Akers Allen

THORNLESS ROSES

"No rose may bloom without a thorn?"
   Come down the garden path and see
How lightly in the scented air
   They bloom for you and me!

See how like rosy clouds, they lie
   Against the perfect, stainless blue!
See how they toss their airy heads,
   And smile for me, for you!

No scanty largess, meanly doled,—
   No pallid blooms, by two, by three,
But a whole crowd of pink-white wings
   Fluttering for you and me.

So fair they are I cannot choose;
   I pluck the rich spoils here and there;
I heap them on your waiting arms;
   I twine them in your hair.

There is no thorn among them all,—
   No sharp sting in the heart of bliss,—
No bitter in the honeyed cup,—
   No burning in the kiss.

Nay, quote the proverb if you must,
   And mock the truth you will not see;
Nathless, Love's thornless roses blow
   Somewhere for you and me.

Julia C. R. Dorr

LOVE ME NOT, LOVE, FOR THAT I FIRST LOVED THEE

***

Love me not, Love, for that I first loved thee,
   Nor love me, Love, for thy sweet pity's sake,
   In knowledge of the mortal pain and ache
   Which is the fruit of love's blood-veined tree.
Let others for my love give love to me:
   From other souls, oh, gladly will I take,
   This burning, heart dry thirst of love to slake,
   What seas of human pity there may be!
Nay, nay, I care no more how love may grow,
   So that I hear thee answer to my call!
   Love me because my piteous tears do flow,
Or that my love for thee did first befall.
   Love me or late or early, fast or slow:
   But love me, Love, for love is one and all!

Richard Watson Gilder

UNTITLED
***

Keep your eyes open when you kiss: do: when
You kiss. All silly time else, close them to;
Unsleeping, I implore you (dear) pursue
In darkness me, as I do you again
Instantly we part . . . only me both then
And when your fingers fall, let there be two
Only, 'in that dream-kingdom': I would have you
Me alone recognize your citizen.

Before who wanted eyes, making love, so?
I do now. However we are driven and hide,
What state we keep all other states condemn,
We see ourselves, we watch the solemn glow
Of empty courts we kiss in . . . Open wide!
You do, you do, and I look into them.

John Berryman

THE LOVER PRAISES
HIS LADY'S BRIGHT BEAUTY

***

Some night I think if you should walk with me
Where the tall trees like ferns on the ocean's floor
Sway slowly in the blue deeps of the moon's flood,
I would put up my hands through that impalpable sea
And tear a branch of stars from the sky, as once I tore
A branch of apple blossoms for you in an April wood.

And I would bend the dewy branch of stars about your little
   head
Till they flamed with pride to be as blossoms amid your hair,
But I would laugh to see them so pale, being near your eyes.
I would say to you, "Love, the Immortals are hovering about
   your head,
They laugh at the dimness of stars in the luminous night of
   your hair."
I would toss that weeping branch back to the mournful skies.

Shaemas O'Sheel

CALYPSO'S SONG TO ULYSSES

My hands are tender feathers,
They can teach your body to soar.
My feet are two comedians
With jokes your flesh has never heard before.

So try to read the meaning
Of the blue veins under my skin
And feel my breasts like gentle wheels
Revolving from your thighs to your chin.

And listen to the rhythm
Of my heartbeat marking the pace
And see the visions sail across
The easy-riding waters of my face.

What is sweeter than the human body?
Two human bodies as they rise and fall.
What is sweeter than two loving bodies?
There is nothing sweeter at all.
Lose yourself, find yourself,
Lose yourself again
On the island of Calypso.

Adrian Mitchell

LOVE POEM

Yours is the face that the earth turns to me.
Continuous beyond its human features lie
The mountain forms that rest against the sky.
With your eyes, the reflecting rainbow, the sun's light
Sees me; forest and flowers, bird and beast
Know and hold me for ever in the world's thought,
Creation's deep untroubled retrospect.

When your hand touches mine, it is the earth
That takes me—the deep grass,
And rocks and rivers; the green graves,
And children still unborn, and ancestors,
In love passed down from hand to hand from God.
Your touch comes from the creation of the world,
From those paternal fingers streaming through the clouds
That break with light the surface of the sea.

Here, where I trace your body with my hand
Love's presence has no end;
For these, your arms that hold me, are the world's.
In us, the continents, clouds and oceans meet
Our arbitrary selves, extensive with the night,
Lost in the heart's worship and the body's sleep.

Kathleen Raine

LOVE SONG

I love my life, but not too well
  To give it to thee like a flower,
So it may pleasure thee to dwell
  Deep in its perfume but an hour.
I love my life, but not too well.

I love my life, but not too well
  To sing it note by note away,
So to thy soul the song may tell
  The beauty of the desolate day.
I love my life, but not too well.

I love my life, but not too well
  To cast it like a cloak on thine,
Against the storms that sound and swell
  Between thy lonely heart and mine
I love my life, but not too well.

Harriet Monroe

BELIEVE ME, IF ALL THOSE ENDEARING YOUNG CHARMS

Believe me, if all those endearing young charms,
   Which I gaze on so fondly to-day,
Were to change by to-morrow, and fleet in my arms,
   Like fairy-gifts fading away,
Thou wouldst still be adored, as this moment thou art,
   Let thy loveliness fade as it will,
And around the dear ruin each wish of my heart
   Would entwine itself verdantly still.

It is not while beauty and youth are thine own,
   And thy cheeks unprofaned by a tear,
That the fervor and faith of a soul may be known,
   To which time will but make thee more dear!
No, the heart that has truly loved never forgets,
   But as truly loves on to the close,
As the sunflower turns to her god when he sets
   The same look which she turned when he rose!

Thomas Moore

THE SWEETEST FLOWER THAT BLOWS

The sweetest flower that blows
   I give you as we part;
For you it is a rose;
   For me it is my heart.

The fragrance it exhales
   (Ah, if you only knew!),
Which but in dying fails,
   It is my love of you.

The sweetest flower that grows
   I give you as we part;
You think it but a rose;
   Ah, me! it is my heart.

Frederick Peterson

SERENADE AT NOONDAY

I do not love you, no, nor all your beauty,
Nor have I fear of your so delicate magics:
I only love the silence that around you
Makes a low twilight.

Yet I desire that thunderous storms of passion
For all I am should surge and clamour through you—
Scattering your follies and your delicate secrets—
Shaking your twilight.

That like a temple bell across the darkness
I should forever echo in your spirit
With tones of legend and of high disaster
Haunting your silence.

Arthur Davison Ficke

STRAWBERRIES

There were never strawberries
like the ones we had
that sultry afternoon
sitting on the step
of the open french window
facing each other
your knees held in mine
the blue plates in our laps
the strawberries glistening
in the hot sunlight
we dipped them in sugar
looking at each other
not hurrying the feast
for one to come
the empty plates
laid on the stone together
with the two forks crossed
and I bent towards you
sweet in that air
in my arms
abandoned like a child
from your eager mouth
the taste of strawberries
in my memory
lean back again
let me love you
let the sun beat
on our forgetfulness
one hour of all
the heat intense

and summer lightning
on the Kilpatrick hills
let the storm wash the plates

Edwin Morgan

CORINNA IN VENDOME

Darling, each morning a blooded rose
Lures the sunlight in, and shows
Her soft, moist and secret part.
See now, before you go to bed,
Her skirts replaced, her deeper red—
A colour much like yours, dear heart.

Alas, her petals will blow away,
Her beauties in a single day
Vanish like ashes on the wind.
O savage Time! that what we prize
Should flutter down before our eyes—
Who also, late or soon, descend.

Then scatter, darling, your caresses
While you may, and wear green dresses;
Gather roses, gather me—
Tomorrow, aching for your charms,
Death shall take you in his arms
And shatter your virginity.

Pierre de Ronsard

SONG

Love me because I am lost;
Love me that I am undone.
That is brave,—no man has wished it,
Not one.

Be strong, to look on my heart
As others look on my face.
Love me,—I tell you that it is a ravaged
Terrible place.

Louise Bogan

LOVE SONG

There is a strong wall about me to protect me:
It is built of the words you have said to me.

There are swords about me to keep me safe:
They are the kisses of your lips.

Before me goes a shield to guard me from harm:
It is the shadow of your arms between me and danger.

All the wishes of my mind know your name,
And the white desires of my heart
They are acquainted with you.
The cry of my body for completeness,
That is a cry to you.
My blood beats out your name to me, unceasing, pitiless—
Your name, your name.

Mary Carolyn Davies

BEFORE YOU CAME
∗
∗∗

Before you came
A word you said
Ran through my days
Like living flame.

It was not you—
It was a name
For loveliness . . .
And yet it drew

Your Self for me
So that I knew
Your mood, your smile,
All you must be.

Oh, long ago
I dreamed you so—
Subtle as flame,

And cold as frost,
And mine, and lost
Before you came.

Marjorie Meeker

LOVE SONG

What have I to say to you
When we shall meet?
Yet—
I lie here thinking of you.

The stain of love
Is upon the world!
Yellow, yellow, yellow
It eats into the leaves,
Smears with saffron
The horned branches that lean
Heavily
Against a smooth purple sky!

There is no light
Only a honey-thick stain
That drips from leaf to leaf
And limb to limb,
Spoiling the colors
Of the whole world—

I am alone.
The weight of love
Has buoyed me up
Till my head
Knocks against the sky.

See me!
My hair is dripping with nectar—

Starlings carry it
On their black wings.

See, at last
My arms and my hands
Are lying idle.

How can I tell
If I shall ever love you again
As I do now?

William Carlos Williams

LOVE PURSUED

Art thou gone in haste?
   I'll not forsake thee;
Runn'st thou ne'er so fast,
   I'll o'ertake thee:
O'er the dales, o'er the downs,
   Through the green meadows,
From the fields through the towns,
   To the dim shadows.

All along the plains,
   To the low fountains,
Up and down agen
   From the high mountains;
Echo then, shall agen
   Tell her I follow,
And the floods to the woods
   Carry my holla, holla, *ce, la, ho, ho, hu.*

Anonymous

THEE, THEE, ONLY THEE

The dawning of morn, the daylight's sinking,
The night's long hours still find me thinking
    Of thee, thee, only thee.
When friends are met, and goblets crown'd,
  And smiles are near that once enchanted,
Unreach'd by all that sunshine round,
  My soul, like some dark spot, is haunted
    By thee, thee, only thee.

Whatever in fame's high path could waken
My spirit once is now forsaken
    For thee, thee, only thee.
Like shores by which some headlong bark
  To the ocean hurries, resting never,
Life's scenes go by me, bright or dark
  I know not, heed not, hastening ever
    To thee, thee, only thee.

I have not a joy but of thy bringing,
And pain itself seems sweet when springing
    From thee, thee, only thee.
Like spells that nought on earth can break,
  Till lips that known the charm have spoken,
This heart, howe'er the world may wake
  Its grief, its scorn, can but be broken
    By thee, thee, only thee.

Thomas Moore

A SONG OF A YOUNG LADY TO HER ANCIENT LOVER

Ancient person, for whom I
All the flattering youth defy,
Long be it ere thou grow old,
Aching, shaking, crazy, cold;
   But still continue as thou art,
   Ancient person of my heart.

On thy withered lips and dry,
Which like barren furrows lie,
Brooding kisses I will pour
Shall thy youthful heat restore
(Such kind showers in autumn fall,
And a second spring recall);
   Nor from thee will ever part,
   Ancient person of my heart.

Thy nobler part, which but to name
In our sex would be counted shame,
By age's frozen grasp possessed,
From his ice shall be released,
And smoothed by my reviving hand,
In former warmth and vigor stand.
All a lover's wish can reach
For thy joy my love shall teach,
And for thy pleasure shall improve
All that art can add to love.
   Yet still I love thee without art,
   Ancient person of my heart.

   John Wilmot

THE KISS

Give me, my love, that billing kiss
   I taught you one delicious night,
When, turning epicures in bliss,
   We tried inventions of delight.

Come, gently steal my lips along
   And let your lips in murmurs move,—
Ah, no!—again—that kiss was wrong—
   How can you be so dull, my love?

"Cease, cease!" the blushing girl replied—
   And in her milky arms she caught me—
"How can you thus your pupil chide;
   You know *'twas in the dark* you taught me!"

Thomas Moore

THE SEA-SHELL

"Listen, darling, and tell me
What the murmurer says to thee,
Murmuring 'twixt a song and a moan,
Changing neither tune nor tone."

"Yes, I hear it,—far and faint,
Like thin-drawn prayer of drowsy saint;
Like the falling of sleep on a weary brain,
When the fevered heart is quiet again."

"By smiling lips and fixed eye,
You are hearing more than song or sigh;
The wrinkled thing has curious ways—
I want to know what words it says."

"I hear a wind on a boatless main
Sigh like the last of a vanishing pain;
On the dreaming waters dreams the moon,
But I hear no words in the murmured tune."

"If it does not say that I love thee well,
'T is a senseless, ill-curved, worn-out shell;
If it is not of love, why sight or sing?
'T is a common, mechanical, useless thing."

"It whispers of love—'t is a prophet shell—
Of a peace that comes and all shall be well;
It speaks not a word of your love to me,
But it tells me to love you eternally."

George MacDonald

HAPPY ARE THEY WHO KISS THEE

Happy are they who kiss thee, morn and even,
Parting the hair upon thy forehead white;
For them the sky is bluer and more bright,
And purer their thanksgivings rise to Heaven.
Happy are they to whom thy songs are given;
Happy are they on whom thy hands alight;
And happiest they for whom thy prayers at night
In tender pity so oft have striven.
Away with vain regrets and selfish sighs—
Even I, dear friend, am lonely, not unblest;
Permitted sometimes on that form to gaze,
Or feel the light of those consoling eyes;
If but a moment on my cheek it stays,
I know that gentle beam from all the rest!

Aubrey De Vere

SUDDEN LIGHTS
***

I have been here before,
   But when or how I cannot tell:
I know the grass beyond the door,
   The sweet keen smell,
The sighing sound, the lights around the shore.

You have been mine before,—
   How long ago I may not know:
But just when at that swallows's soar
   Your neck turned so,
Some veil did fall,—I knew it all of yore.

Has this been thus before?
   And shall not thus time's eddying flight
Still with our lives our love restore
   In death's despite,
And day and night yield one delight once more?

Dante Gabriel Rossetti

AN HOUR WITH THEE

An hour with thee! When earliest day
Dapples with gold the eastern grey,
Oh, what can frame my mind to bear
The toil and turmoil, cark and care,
New griefs, which coming hours unfold,
And sad remembrance of the old?
   One hour with thee.

One hour with thee! When burning June
Waves his red flag at pitch of noon;
What shall repay the faithful swain,
His labour on the sultry plain;
And, more than cave or sheltering bough,
Cool feverish blood and throbbing brow?
   One hour with thee.

One hour with thee! When sun is set,
Oh, what can teach me to forget
The thankless labours of the day;
The hopes, the wishes, flung away;
The increasing wants, and lessening gains,
The master's pride, who scorns my pains?
   One hour with thee.

Walter Scott

THE PASSIONATE SHEPHERD
TO HIS LOVE

Come live with me and be my love
And we will all the pleasures prove
That hills and valleys, dales and fields,
And all the craggy mountains yields.

And we will sit upon the rocks
And see the shepherds feed their flocks
By shallow rivers, to whose falls
Melodious birds sing madrigals.

And I will make thee beds of roses
And a thousand fragrant posies,
A cap of flowers, and a kirtle
Embroidered all with leaves of myrtle,

A gown made of the finest wool,
Which from our pretty lambs we pull,
Fair-lined slippers for the cold
With buckles of the purest gold,

A belt of straw and ivy-buds
With coral clasps and amber studs.
And if these pleasures may thee move,
Come live with me and be my love.

Thy silver dishes for thy meat,
As precious as the gods do eat,
Shall on an ivory table be
Prepared each day for thee and me.

The shepherd swains shall dance and sing
For thy delight each May morning.
If these delights thy mind may move,
Then live with me and be my love.

Christopher Marlowe

RONDO
*

Did I love thee? I only did desire
To hold thy body unto mine,
And smite it with strange fire
Of kisses burning as a wine,
And catch thy odorous hair, and twine
It thro' my fingers amorously.
   Did I love thee?

Did I love thee? I only did desire
To watch thine eyelids lilywise
Closed down, and thy warm breath respire
As it came through the thickening sighs,
And speak my love in such fair guise
Of passion's sobbing agony.
   Did I love thee?

Did I love thee? I only did desire
To drink the perfume of thy blood
In vision, and thy senses tire
Seeing them shift from ebb to flood
In consonant sweet interlude,
And if love such a thing not be,
   I loved not thee.

George Moore

ENTRY APRIL 28

*
**

Because hate is legislated . . . written into the primer and
 the testament,
shot into our blood and brain like vaccine or vitamins

Because our day is of time, of hours—and the clock-hand turns,
closes the circle upon us: and black timeless night
sucks us in like quicksand, receives us totally—
without a raincheck or a parachute, a key to heaven or the
 last long look

I need love more than ever now . . . I need your love,
I need love more than hope or money, wisdom or a drink

Because the slow negative death withers the world—and only
 yes
can turn the tide
Because love has your face and body . . . and your hands
 are tender
and your mouth is sweet—and God has made no other eyes
 like yours.

Walter Benton

UNTITLED

Ah, I remember well—and how can I
But ever more remember well—when first
Our flame began, when scare we knew what was
The flame we felt; when as we sat and sighed,
And looked upon each other, and conceived
Not what we ailed, yet something we did ail,
And yet were well, and yet we were not well,
And what was our disease we could not tell.
Then would we kiss, then sigh, then look: and thus
In that first garden of our simpleness
We spent our childhood: but when years began
To reap the fruit of knowledge, ah, how then
Would she with graver looks, with sweet stern brow,
Check my presumption and my forwardness;
Yet still would give me flowers, still would me shew
What she would have me, yet not have me, know.

Samuel Daniel

FROM INDOLENCE: XII
***

Thou didst delight my eyes:
Yet who am I? nor first
Nor last nor best, that durst
Once dream of thee for prize;
Nor this the only time
Thou shalt set love to rhyme.

Thou didst delight my ear:
Ah! little praise; thy voice
makes other hearts rejoice,
Makes all ears glad that hear;
And short my joy; but yet,
O song, do not forget!

For what wert thou to me?
How shall I say? The moon,
That poured her midnight noon
Upon his wrecking sea;—
A sail that for a day
Has cheered the castaway.

Robert Bridges

I'LL NEVER LOVE THEE MORE

My dear and only love, I pray
   That little world of thee
Be governed by no other sway
   Than purest monarchy;
For if confusion have a part
   (Which virtuous souls abhor),
And hold a synod in thine heart,
   I'll never love thee more.

Like Alexander I will reign,
   And I will reign alone;
My thoughts did evermore disdain
   A rival on my throne.
He either fears his fate too much,
   Or his deserts are small,
That does not put it to the touch,
   To gain or lose it all.

And in the empire of thine heart,
   Where I should solely be,
If others do pretend a part
   Or dare to vie with me,
Or if Committees thou erect,
   And go on such a score,
I'll laugh and sing at thy neglect,
   And never love thee more.

But if thou wilt prove faithful then,
   And constant of thy word,
I'll make thee glorious by my pen

And famous by my sword;
I'll serve thee in such noble ways
  Was never heard before;
I'll crown and deck thee all with bays,
  And love thee more and more.

James Graham

BECAUSE
***

It is not because your heart is mine—mine only—
    Mine alone,
It is not because you choose me weak and lonely
    For your own;
Not because the earth is fairer, and the skies
    Spread above you
Are more radiant for the shining of your eyes—
    That I love you!

It is not because the world's perplexèd meaning
    Grows more clear;
And the Parapets of Heaven, with angels leaning,
    Seem more near;
And Nature sings of praise with all her voices
    Since yours spoke,
Since within my silent heart, that now rejoices,
    Love awoke!

Nay, not even because your hand holds heart and life,
    At your will
Soothing, hushing all its discord, making strife
    Calm and still;
Teaching Trust to fold her wings, nor ever roam
    From her nest;
Teaching Love that her securest, safest home
    Must be Rest.

But because this human Love, though true and sweet,—
　Yours and mine,—
Has been sent by Love more tender, more complete,
　More divine,
That it leads our hearts to rest at last in Heaven,
　Far above you;
Do I take you as a gift that God has given—
　And I love you!

Adelaide Anne Procter

PSALM TO MY BELOVED

Lo, I have opened unto you the wide gates of my being,
And like a tide you have flowed into me.
The innermost recesses of my spirit are full of you, and all
    the channels of my soul are grown sweet with your presence.
For you have brought me peace;
The peace of great tranquil waters, and the quiet of the summer
    sea.
Your hands are filled with peace as the noon-tide is filled with
    light; about your head is bound the eternal quiet of the stars,
    and in your heart dwells the calm miracle of twilight.
I am utterly content.
In all my spirit is no ripple of unrest,
For I have opened unto you the wide gates of my being
And like a tide you have flowed into me.

Eunice Tietjens

REST

As a little child I come
To be gathered to your breast
So tired that my lips are dumb,
So sad that my warm heart is numb:
   Belovèd, let me rest.

Oh, how all the noises die,
All the cruel voices cease,
I can sleep when you are by,
And I am too faint to cry:
   Here at last is peace.

Hold me, nurse me, love me . . . so . . .
Almost I could learn to weep!
Hush, I feel my spirit grow . . .
When you tire . . . let me go . . .
   I shall be . . . asleep.

Irene Rutherford McLeod

TO HIS MISTRESS

My light thou art, without thy glorious sight
My eyes are darkened with eternal night;
My love, thou art my way, my life, my light.

Thou art my way, I wander if thou fly;
Thou art my light, if hid, how blind am I!
Thou art my life, if thou withdraw'st I die

Thou art my life, if thou but turn away,
My life's a thousand deaths. Thou art my way;
Without thee, love, I travel not, but stray.

John Wilmot

UNTITLED
✸
✸✸

"I'm sorry that I spelt the word,
   I hate to go above you,
Because"—the brown eyes lower fell—
   "Because, you see, I love you!"

John Greenleaf Whittier

THE LYRIC
***

The wandering airs they faint
On the dark, the silent stream—
The Champak odors fail
Like sweet thoughts in a dream;
The nightingale's complaint,
It dies upon her heart;—
As I must on thine,
Oh, belovèd as thou art!

Oh lift me from the grass!
I die! I faint! I fail!
Let thy love in kisses rain
On my lips and eyelids pale.
My cheek is cold and white, alas!
My heart beats loud and fast;—
Oh! press it to thine own again,
Where it will break at last.

Percy Bysshe Shelley

BELOVED, MY BELOVED, WHEN I THINK

Belovèd, my belovèd, when I think
That thou wast in the world a year ago,
What time I sat alone here in the snow,
And saw no footprint, heard the silence sink
No moment at thy voice, but link by link,
Went counting all my chains as if that so
They never could fall off at any blow
Struck by thy possible hand,—why, thus I drink
Of life's great cup of wonder! Wonderful,
Never to feel thee thrill the day or night
With, personal act or speech, nor ever cull
Some prescience of thee with the blossoms white
Thou sawest growing! Atheists are as dull,
Who cannot guess God's presence out of sight.

Elizabeth Barrett Browning

IF THOU MUST LOVE ME, LET IT BE FOR NOUGHT

If thou must love me, let it be for nought
Except for love's sake only. Do not say,
"I love her for her smile, her look, her way
Of speaking gently, for a trick of thought
That falls in well with mine, and certes brought
A sense of pleasant ease on such a day";
For these things in themselves, belovèd, may
Be changed, or change for thee: and love so wrought
May be unwrought so. Neither love me for
Thine own dear pity's wiping my cheeks dry:
A creature might forget to weep, who bore
Thy comfort long, and lose thy love thereby.
But love me for love's sake, that evermore
Thou mayst love on through love's eternity.

Elizabeth Barrett Browning

SONNET XLIII, FROM THE PORTUGUESE

How do I love thee? Let me count the ways.
I love thee to the depth and breadth and height
My soul can reach, when feeling out of sight
For the ends of Being and ideal Grace.
I love thee to the level of every day's
Most quiet need, by sun and candlelight.
I love thee freely, as men strive for Right;
I love thee purely, as they turn from Praise.
I love thee with the passion put to use
In my old griefs, and with my childhood's faith.
I love thee with a love I seemed to lose
With my lost saints,—I love thee with the breath,
Smiles, tears, of all my life!—and, if God choose,
I shall but love thee better after death.

Elizabeth Barrett Browning

UNTITLED
***

Love me little, love me long,
Is the burden of my song.
Love that is too hot and strong
   Burneth soon to waste:
Still I would not have thee cold,
Not too backward, nor too bold;
Love that lasteth til 'tis old
   Fadeth not in haste.
    Love me little, love me long,
    Is the burden of my song.

If thou lovest me too much,
It will not prove as true as touch;
Love me little, more than such,
   For I fear the end:
I am with little well content,
And a little from thee sent
Is enough, with true intent
   To be steadfast friend.
    Love me little, love me long,
    Is the burden of my song.

Say thou lov'st me while thou live,
I to thee my love will give,
Never dreaming to deceive
   Whiles that life endures:
Nay, and after death, in sooth,
I to thee will keep my truth,
As now when in my May of youth;
   This my love assures.
    Love me little, love me long,
    Is the burden of my song.

Constant love is moderate ever,
And it will through life persèver:

Give me that, with true endeavour
   I will it restore.
A suit of durance let it be
For all weathers that for me
For the land or for the sea,
   Lasting evermore.
    Love me little, love me long,
    Is the burden of my song.

Winter's cold or summer's heat,
Autumn tempests, on it beat,
It can never know defeat,
   Never can rebel:
Such the love that I would gain,
Such the love, I tell thee plain,
Thou must give, or woo in vain:
   So to thee farewell.
    Love me little, love me long,
    Is the burden of my song.

                  Anonymous

SONNET

Trust me, I have not earned your dear rebuke;
   I love, as you would have me, God the most;
   Would love not you, but Him, must one be lost,
Nor with Lot's wife cast back a faithless look,
Unready to forego what I forsook.
   This say I, having counted up the cost;
   This though I be the feeblest of God's host;
The sorriest sheep Christ shepherds with His crook.
Yet while I love my God the most, I deem
   That I can never love you overmuch;
     I love Him more, so let me love you too.
   Yea, as I apprehend it, love is such
I cannot love you if I love not Him,
   I cannot love Him if I love you not.

Christina Georgina Rossetti

LOVE

Love? I will tell thee what it is to love!
   It is to build with human thoughts a shrine
Where hope sits brooding like a beauteous dove;
   Where Time seems young, and Life a thing divine.
   All tastes, all pleasures, all desires combine
To consecrate this sanctuary of bliss.
   Above, the stars in cloudless beauty shine;
Around, the streams their flowery margins kiss;
And if there's heaven on earth, that heaven is surely this.

Yes, this is Love, the steadfast and the true,
   The immortal glory which hath never set;
The best, the brightest boon the heart e'er knew:
   Of all life's sweets the very sweetest yet!
   O! who but can recall the eve they met,
To breathe, in some green walk, their first young vow?
   While summer flowers with moonlight dews were wet,
And winds sighed soft around the mountain's brow,
And all was rapture then which is but memory now!

Charles Swain

BEDOUIN SONG

From the desert I come to thee
　On a stallion shod with fire;
And the winds are left behind
　In the speed of my desire.
Under thy window I stand
　And the midnight hears my cry:
I love thee, I love but thee,
　　With a love that cannot die
　　　Till the sun grows cold,
　　　And the stars are old,
　　　And the leaves of the Judgment Book unfold!

Look from thy window and see
　My passion and my pain;
I lie on the sands below
　And I faint in thy disdain.
Let the night-winds touch thy brow
　With the heat of my burning sigh,
And melt thee to hear the vow
　Of a love that shall not die
　　　Till the sun grows cold,
　　　And the stars are old,
　　　And the leaves of the Judgment Book unfold!

My steps are nightly driven
　By the fever in my breast
To hear from thy lattice breathed
　The word that shall give me rest.
Open the door of thy heart
　And open thy chamber door,

And my kisses shall teach thy lips
   The love that shall fade no more
      Till the sun grows cold,
      And the stars are old,
      And the leaves of the Judgment Book unfold!

                              Bayard Taylor

CONSTANCY

Were I as base as is the lowly plain,
And you, my love, as high as heaven above,
Yet should the thoughts of me, your humble swain,
Ascend to heaven in honour of my love.
Were I as high as heaven above the plain,
And you, my love, as humble and as low
As are the deepest bottoms of the main,
Whereso'er you were, with you my love should go.
Were you the earth, dear love, and I the skies,
My love should shine on you, like to the sun,
And look upon you with ten thousand eyes,
Till heaven wax'd blind, and till the world were done.
   Whereso'er I am, below,—or else above you,—
   Whereso'er you are, my heart shall truly love you.

Joshua Sylvester

HOW MANY TIMES

How many times do I love thee, dear?
   Tell me how many thoughts there be
     In the atmosphere
     Of a new-fallen year,
Whose white and sable hours appear
   The latest flake of Eternity:
So many times do I love thee, dear.

How many times do I love, again?
   Tell me how many beads there are
     In a silver chain
     Of the evening rain,
Unravelled from the tumbling main,
   And threading the eye of a yellow star:
So many times do I love, again

Thomas Lovell Beddoes

OBLATION

Ask nothing more of me, sweet;
  All I can give you I give;
  Heart of my heart, were it more,
More should be laid at your feet:
  Love that should help you to live,—
    Song that should spur you to soar.

All things were nothing to give,
  Once to have sense of you more,—
  Touch you and taste of you, sweet,
Think you and breathe you, and live
  Swept of your wings as they soar,
    Trodden by chance of your feet.

I, who have love and no more,
  Bring you but love of you, sweet.
    He that hath more, let him give;
He that hath wings, let him soar:
  Mine is the heart at your feet
    Here, that must love you to live.

Algernon Charles Swinburne

UNTITLED
*
**

I will make you brooches and toys for your delight
Of bird-song at morning and star-shine at night.
I will make a place fit for you and me
Of green days in forest and blue days at sea.

I will make my kitchen, and you shall keep your room,
Where white flows the river and bright blows the broom,
And you shall wash your linen and keep your body white
In rainfall at morning and dewfall at night.

And this shall be for music when no one else is near,
The fine song for singing, the rare song to hear!
That only I remember, that only you admire,
Of the broad road that stretches and the roadside fire.

Robert Louis Stevenson

SONNET

Yet, love, mere love, is beautiful indeed
And worthy of acceptation. Fire is bright,
Let temple burn, or flax; and equal light
Leaps in the flame from cedar-plank or weed:
And love is fire. And when I say at need
I love thee . . . mark! . . . I love thee—in thy sight
I stand transfigured, glorified aright,
With conscience of the new rays that proceed
Out of my face toward thine. There's nothing low
In love, when love the lowest: meanest creatures
Who love God, God accepts while loving so.
And what I *feel*, across the inferior features
Of what I *am*, doth flash itself, and show
How that great work of Love enhances Nature's.

Elizabeth Barrett Browning

SONG FROM A DRAMA

I know not if moonlight or starlight
   Be soft on the land and the sea,—
I catch but the near light, the far light,
   Of eyes that are beaming for me;
The scent of the night, of the roses,
   May burden the air for thee, Sweet,—
'Tis only the breath of thy sighing
   I know as I lie at thy feet.

The winds may be sobbing or singing,
   Their touch may be fervent or cold,
The night bells may toll or be ringing,—
   I care not while thee I enfold!
The feast may go on, and the music
   Be scattered in ecstasy round,—
Thy whisper, "I love thee! I love thee!"
   Hath flooded my soul with its sound.

I think not of time that is flying,
   How short is the hour I have won,
How near is this living to dying,
   How the shadow still follows the sun;
There is naught upon earth, no desire
   Worth a thought, though 't were had by a sign!
I love thee! I love thee! bring nigher
   Thy spirit, thy kisses, to mine.

Edmund Clarence Stedman

MEASURE FOR MEASURE

What love do I bring you? The earth
   Full of love were far lighter;
The great hollow sky full of love
   Something slighter.

Earth full and heaven full were less
   Than the full measure given:
Nay, say a heart full,—the heart
   Holds earth and heaven!

Harriet Prescott Spofford

FORGET THEE

"Forget thee?" If to dream by night, and muse on thee by day,
If all the worship, deep and wild, a poet's heart can pay,
If prayers in absence breathed for thee to Heaven's protecting power,
If winged thoughts that flit to thee—a thousand in an hour,
If busy Fancy blending thee with all my future lot,
If this thou call'st "forgetting," thou indeed shalt be forgot!

"Forget thee?" Bid the forest birds forget their sweetest tune;
"Forget thee?" Bid the sea forget to swell beneath the moon;
Bid the thirsty flowers to drink, the eve's refreshing dew;
Thyself forget thine "own dear land," and its "mountains wild and blue;"
Forget each old familiar face, each long-remembered spot;
When these things are forgot by thee, then thou shalt be forgot!

Keep, if thou wilt, thy maiden peace, still calm and fancy free,
For God forbid thy gladsome heart should grow less glad for me;
Yet, while that heart is still unwon, O, bid not mine to rove,
But let it nurse its humble faith and uncomplaining love,
If these, preserved for patient years, at last avail me not,
Forget me, then;—but ne'er believe that thou canst be forgot!

John Moultrie

UNTITLED
***

O Beauty, passing beauty! sweetest Sweet!
 How canst thou let me waste my youth in sighs?
I only ask to sit beside thy feet.
 Thou knowest I dare not look into thine eyes.
Might I but kiss thy hand! I dare not fold
 My arms about thee—scarcely dare to speak.
And nothing seems to me so wild and bold,
 As with one kiss to touch thy blessed cheek.
Methinks if I should kiss thee, no control
 Within the thrilling brain could keep afloat,
 The subtle spirit. Even while I spoke,
The bare word KISS hath made my inner soul
 To tremble like a lustering, ere the note
 Hath melted in the silence that it broke.

Alfred, Lord Tennyson

UNTITLED
***

My love is like a red red rose
That's newly sprung in June:
My love is like the melodie
That's sweetly played in tune.

As fair art thou, my bonnie lass,
So deep in love am I:
And I will love thee still, my dear,
Till a' the seas gang dry.

Till a' the seas gang dry, my dear,
And the rocks melt wi' the sun:
And I will love thee still, my dear,
While the sands o' life shall run.

And fare thee weel, my only love,
And fare thee weel a while!
And I will come again, my love,
Tho' it were ten thousand mile.

Robert Burns

UNTITLED
***

Winding all my life about thee,
   Let me lay my lips on thine;
What is all the world without thee,
   Mine—oh mine!

Let me press my heart out on thee,
   Crush it like a fiery vine,
Spilling sacramental on thee
   Love's red wine,

Let thy strong eyes yearning o'er me
   Draw me with their force divine;
All my soul has gone before me
   Clasping thine.

Irresistibly I follow
   As wherever we may run
Runs our shadow, as the swallow
   Seeks the sun.

Yea, I tremble, swoon, surrender
   All my spirit to thy sway
As a star is drowned in splendour
   Of the day.

Mathilde Blind

IS IT A SIN TO LOVE THEE?
*
**

Is it a sin to love thee? Then my soul is deeply dyed,
For my lifeblood, as it gushes, takes its crimson from love's tide;
And I feel its waves roll o'er me and the blushes mount my brow,
And my pulses quicken wildly, as the love dreams come and go:
I feel my spirit's weakness; I know my spirit's power;
I have felt my proud heart struggle in temptation's trying hour;
Yet, amid the din of conflict, bending o'er life's hallowed shrine,
Yielding all, my soul had murmured, I am thine, forever thine!

Is it a sin to love thee? What were existence worth,
Bereft of all the heaven that lingers still on earth!
Friendship's smiles, like gleams of sunlight, shed their feeling o'er the heart,
But the soul still cries for something more than friendship can impart.
Frozen hearts, like ice-bound eyries, that no summer ray can melt,
Vainly boast their power to conquer what their hearts have never felt;
But envy not their glory, 'mid the rapture that is mine,
When with earnest soul I tell thee I am thine, forever thine!

Is it a sin to love thee? Gentle voices round me fall,
And I press warm hearts about me—but I've given thee my all.
What though stern fate divides us, and our hands, not hearts, be riven—
My all of earth thou hast—wilt more? I dare not offer heaven!
But in some blessed moment, when our dark eyes flashing meet,

When I feel thy power so near me, feel thy heart's quick pulses
   beat,
Then I know—may God forgive me!—I would everything resign
All I have, or all I hope for—to be thine—forever thine.

Is it a sin to love thee? I remember well the hour
When we would our love to conquer, resist temptations' power;
When I felt my heart was breaking and my all of life was
   gone;
When I wept the hour I met thee, and the hour that I was
   born;
But a hidden storm was raging, and amid the muffled din
I flung my arms upon thy bosom, with thy warm hands clasped
   in mine,
I smiled through tears and murmured: I am thine, forever thine.

Is it a sin to love thee? with love's signet on thy brow?
Though thy lot be dark as Hades I'll cling to thee as now;
Not mine the heart to fail thee, when other cheeks grow pale;
We have shared the storm together; I'll stand by thee through
   the gale.
Though our bark may drift asunder, yet, with true hearts
   beating high,
Let the golden sunlight cheer us, or the angry storm clouds
   fly.
From our helms with steady brightness our beacon lights shall
   shine,
And the watchwords on our pennons shall be—thine, forever
   thine.

Is it a sin to love thee? When I bend my knees in prayer,
And before a High Omniscience my burdened heart lay bare,
On the breath of love to heaven ascends thy blessed name,
And I plead weak and erring nature, if loving thee be shame.
Heaven knows 'tis no light sacrifices I've offered up to thee,
No gilded dreams of fancy, but my being's destiny.
Since our fates we may not conquer here, divided thy lot from
    mine—
In the starlit world above us, call me thine—forever thine!

Anonymous

IF YOU BUT KNEW

If you but knew
How all my days seemed filled with dreams of you,
How sometimes in the silent night
Your eyes thrill through me with their tender light,
How oft I hear your voice when others speak,
How you 'mid other forms I seek—
Oh, love more real than though such dreams were true
If you but knew.

Could you but guess
How you alone make all my happiness,
How I am more than willing for your sake
To stand alone, give all and nothing take,
Nor chafe to think you bound while I am free,
Quite free, till death, to love you silently,
Could you but guess.

Could you but learn
How when you doubt my truth I sadly yearn
To tell you all, to stand for one brief space
Unfettered, soul to soul, as face to face,
To crown you king, my king, till life shall end,
My lover and likewise my truest friend,
Would you love me, dearest, as fondly in return,
Could you but learn?

Anonymous

SONG
***

Song is so old,
   Love is so new—
Let me be still
   And kneel to you.

Let me be still
   And breathe no word,
Save what my warm blood
    Sings unheard.

Let my warm blood
   Sing low of you—
Song is so fair,
   Love is so new!

Hermann Hagedorn

IN A ROSE GARDEN

A hundred years from now, dear heart,
   We shall not care at all.
It will not matter then a whit,
   The honey or the gall.
The summer days that we have known
Will all forgotten be and flown;
The garden will be overgrown
   Where now the roses fall.

A hundred years from now, dear heart,
   We shall not mind the pain;
The throbbing crimson tide of life
   Will not have left a stain.
The song we sing together, dear,
The dream we dream together here,
Will mean no more than means a tear
   Amid a summer rain.

A hundred years from now, dear heart,
   The grief will all be o'er;
The sea of care will surge in vain
   Upon a careless shore.
These glasses we turn down to-day
Here at the parting of the way—
We shall be wineless then as they,
   And shall not mind it more.

A hundred years from now, dear heart,
   We'll neither know nor care
What came of all life's bitterness,
   Or followed love's despair.
Then fill the glasses up again,
And kiss me through the rose-leaf rain;
We'll build one castle more in Spain,
   And dream one more dream there.

John Bennett

THE LADDER
**

I had a sudden vision in the night—
I did not sleep, I dare not say I dreamed—
Beside my bed a pallid ladder gleamed
And lifted upward to the sky's dim height:
And every rung shone strangely in that light,
And every rung a woman's body seemed,
Outstretched, and down the sides her long hair streamed,
And you—you climbed that ladder of delight!
You climed, sure-footed, naked rung by rung,
Clasped them and trod them, called them by their name,
And my name too I heard you speak at last;
You stood upon my breast the while and flung
A hand up to the next! And then—oh shame—
I kissed the foot that bruised me as it passed.

Leonora Speyer

A WOMAN'S LAST WORD

*
**

Let's contend no more, Love,
   Strive nor weep:
All be as before, Love,
   —only sleep!

What's so wild as words are?
   I and thou
In debate, as birds are,
   Hawk on bough!

See the creatures stalking
   While we speak!
Hush and hide the talking,
   Cheek on cheek!

What so false as truth is,
   False to thee?
Where the serpent's tooth is,
   Shun the tree—

Where the apple reddens
   Never pry—
Lest we lose our Edens,
   Eve and I!

Be a god and hold me
   With a charm!
Be a man and fold me
   With thine arm!

Teach me, only teach Love!
   As I ought.

I will speak thy speech, Love,
   Think thy thought—

Meet, if thou require it,
   Both demands,
Laying flesh and spirit
   In thy hands.

That shall be tomorrow,
   Not tonight:
I must bury sorrow
   Out of sight:

—Must a little weep, Love,
   (foolish me!)
And so fall asleep, Love,
   Loved by thee.

              Robert Browning

SERENADE
**

Stars of the summer night!
   Far in your azure deeps,
Hide, hide your golden light!
   She sleeps!
My lady sleeps!
   Sleeps!

Moon of the summer night!
   Far down your western steeps,
Sink, sink in silvery light!
   She sleeps!
My lady sleeps!
   Sleeps!

Wind of the summer night!
   Where yonder woodbine creeps,
Fold, fold thy pinions light!
   She sleeps!
My lady sleeps!
   Sleeps!

Dreams of the summer night!
   Tell her, her lover keeps
Watch! while in the slumbers light
   She sleeps!
My lady sleeps!
   Sleeps!

      Henry Wadsworth Longfellow

UNTITLED
***

Or love me less, or love me more,
   And play not with my liberty,
Either take all, or all restore,
   Bind me at least, or set me free;
Let me some nobler torture find
Than of a doubtful wavering mind,
Take all my peace, but you betray
Mine honour too this cruel way.

'Tis true that I have nursed before
   That hope of which I know complain,
And, having little, sought no more,
   Fearing to meet with your disdain:
The sparks of favour you did give
I gently blow to make them live:
And yet have gained by all this care
No rest in hope, nor in despair.

I see you wear that pitying smile
   Which you have still vouchsafed my smart,
Content thus cheaply to beguile
   And entertain a harmless heart:
But I no longer can give way
To hope, which doth so little pay;
And yet I dare no freedom owe
Whilst you are kind, though but in show.

Then give me more or give me less,
   Do not disdain a mutual sense,
Or your unpitying beauties dress
   In their own free indifference
But show not a severer eye
Sooner to give me liberty,
For I shall love the very scorn
Which for my sake you do put on.

Sidney Godolphin

SHE WALKS IN BEAUTY

She walks in beauty, like the night
   Of cloudless climes and starry skies;
And all that's best of dark and bright
   Meet in her aspect and her eyes:
Thus mellowed to that tender light
   Which heaven to gaudy day denies.

One shade the more, one ray the less,
   Had half impaired the nameless grace
Which waves in every raven tress
   Or softly lightens o'er her face;
Where thoughts serenely sweet express
   How pure, how dear their dwelling-place.

And on that cheek, and o'er that brow
   So soft, so calm, yet eloquent,
The smiles that win, the tints that glow,
   But tell of days in goodness spent,
A mind at peace with all below,
   A heart whose love is innocent!

Lord Byron

THERE IS NONE, O NONE BUT YOU

There is none, O none but you,
  That from me estrange the sight,
Whom mine eyes affect to view,
  And chained ears hear with delight.

Other beauties others move:
  In you I all graces find;
Such is the effect of Love,
  To make them happy that are kind.

Women in frail beauty trust,
  Only seem you fair to me:
Still prove truly kind and just,
  For that may not dissembled be.

Sweet, afford me then your sight,
  That, surveying all your looks,
Endless volumes I may write,
  And fill the world with envied books:

Which, when after-ages view,
  All shall wonder and despair,—
Woman, to find a man so true,
  Or man, a woman half so fair!

Thomas Campion

OSSIAN'S SERENADE

Oh, come with me in my little canoe,
Where the sea is calm, and the sky is blue!
Oh, come with me, for I long to go
To those isles where the mango apples grow!
Oh, come with me and be my love!
For thee the jungle depth I'll rove;
I'll gather the honeycomb bright as gold,
And chase the elk to its secret hold.

I'll chase the antelope over the plain,
The tiger's cub I'll bind with a chain,
And the wild gazelle, with its silvery feet,
I'll give thee for a playmate sweet.

I'll climb the palm for the bia's nest,
Red peas I'll gather to deck thy breast;
I'll pierce the cocoa's cup for its wine,
And haste to thee, if thou'lt be mine.
Then come with me in my light canoe,
While the sea is calm and the sky is blue,
For should we linger another day,
Storms may arise and love decay.

Oh, come if the love thou hast for me
Is pure and fresh as mine for thee—
Fresh as the fountain under ground,
When first 'tis by the lapwing found!
Our sands are bare, and down their slope,
The silvery-footed antelope,
As gracefully and gaily springs,
As o'er the marble courts of kings.

Major Calder Campbell

ALONE IN APRIL

Rustling leaves of the willow-tree
Peering downward at you and me,
And no man else in the world to see.

Only the birds, whose dusty coats
Show dark in the green—whose throbbing throats
Turn joy to music and love to notes.

Lean your body against the tree,
Lifting your red lips up to me,
Ettarre, and kiss with no man to see!

And let us laugh for a little.—Yea,
Let love and laughter herald the day
When laughter and love will be put away.

James Branch Cabell

UNTITLED
***

Come away, come, sweet Love!
　　The golden morning breaks;
All the earth, all the air,
　　Of love and pleasures speaks.
Teach thine arms then to embrace,
　　And sweet rosy lips to kiss,

And mix our souls in mutual bliss
Eyes were made for beauty's grace,
　　Viewing, rueing, love's long pain,
　　Procured by beauty's rude disdain.

Come away, come, sweet Love!
　　The golden morning wastes
While the sun, from his sphere,
　　His fiery arrow casts,
Making all the shadows fly,
　　Playing, staying in the grove,
　　To entertain the stealth of love.
Thither, sweet Love, let us hie,
　　Flying, dying in desire,
　　Winged with sweep hopes and heavenly fire.

Come away, come, sweet Love!
　　Do not in vain adorn
Beauty's grace, that should rise
　　Like to the naked morn.
Lilies on the river's side.
　　And fair Cyprian flowers new-blown,
　　Desire no beauties but their own:
Ornament is nurse of pride.
　　Pleasure measure love's delight
　　Haste then, sweet Love, our wishëd flight!

　　　　　　　　　　　Anonymous

NOCTURNE

All the earth a hush of white,
   White with moonlight all the skies;
Wonder of a winter night—
   And . . . your eyes.

Hues no palette dares to claim
   Where the spoils of sunken ships
Leap to light in singing flame—
   And . . . your lips.

Darkness as the shadows creep
   Where the embers sigh to rest;
Silence of a world asleep—
   And . . . your breast.

Amelia Josephine Burr

I WANT YOU

I want you when the shades of eve are falling
    And purpling shadows drift across the land;
When sleepy birds to loving mates are calling—
    I want the soothing softness of your hand.

I want you when the stars shine up above me,
    And Heaven's flooded with the bright moonlight;
I want you with your arms and lips to love me
    Throughout the wonder watches of the night.

I want you when in dreams I still remember
    The ling'ring of your kiss—for old times' sake—
With all your gentle ways, so sweetly tender,
    I want you in the morning when I wake.

I want you when the day is at its noontime,
    Sun-steeped and quiet, or drenched with sheets of rain;
I want you when the roses bloom in June-time;
    I want you when the violets came again.

I want you when my soul is thrilled with passion;
    I want you when I'm weary and depressed;
I want you when I'm lazy, slumbrous fashion
    My senses need the haven of your breast.

I want you when through field and woods I'm roaming;
    I want you when I'm standing on the shore;
I want you when the summer birds are homing—
    And when they've flown—I want you more and more.

I want you dear, through every changing season;
   I want you with a tear or with a smile;
I want you more than any rhyme or reason—
   I want you, want you, want you—all the while.

Arthur L. Gillom

NOW WHAT IS LOVE

Now what is Love, I pray thee, tell?
   It is that fountain and that well
     Where pleasure and repentance dwell;
   It is, perhaps, the sauncing bell
   That tolls all into heaven or hell;
   And this is Love, as I hear tell.

Yet what is Love, I prithee, say?
   It is a work on holiday,
   It is December matched with May,
   When lusty bloods in fresh array
   Hear ten months after of the play;
   And this is Love, as I hear say.

Yet what is Love, good shepherd, sain?
   It is a sunshine mixed with rain,
   It is a toothache or like pain,
   It is a game where none hath gain;
   The lass saith no, yet would full fain;
   And this is Love, as I hear sain.

Yet, shepherd, what is Love, I pray?
   It is a yes, it is a nay,
   A pretty kind of sporting fray,
   It is a thing will soon away.
   Then, nymphs, take vantage while ye may;
   And this is Love, as I hear say.

Yet what is Love, good shepherd, show?
   A thing that creeps, it cannot go,
   A prize that passeth to and fro,
   A thing for one, a thing for moe,
   And he that proves shall find it so;
   And shepherd, this is Love, I trow.

Walter Raleigh

AH, HOW SWEET IT IS TO LOVE!

Ah, how sweet it is to love!
   Ah how gay is young Desire!
And what pleasing pains we prove
   When we first approach Love's fire!
Pains of Love can be sweeter far
Than all other pleasures are.

Sighs which are from lovers blown
   Do but gently heave the heart:
Even the tears they shed alone
   Cure, like trickling balm, their smart:
Lovers, when they lose their breath,
Bleed away in easy death.

Love and Time with reverance use,
   Treat them like a parting friend;
Nor the golden gifts refuse
   Which in youth sincere they send:
For each year their price is more,
And they less simple than before.

Love, like spring-tides full and high,
   Swells in every youthful vein;
But each tide does less supply,
   Till they quite shrink in again:
If a flow in age appear,
'Tis but rain, and runs not clear.

John Dryden

YOU KISSED ME

You kissed me! My head drooped low on your breast
With a feeling of shelter and infinite rest,
While the holy emotion my tongue dared not speak,
Flashed up as in flame, from my heart to my cheek;
Your arms held me fast; oh! your arms were so bold—
Heart beat against heart in their passions fold.
Your glances seemed drawing my soul through mine eyes,
As the sun draws the mist from the sea to the skies.
Your lips clung to mine till I prayed in my bliss.
They might never unclasp from the rapturous kiss.

You kissed me! My heart, my breath and my will
In delirious joy for a moment stood still.
Life had for me then no temptations, no charms,
No visions of rapture outside of your arms;
And were I this instant an angel possessed
Of the peace and the joy that belong to the blest,
I would fling my white robes unrepiningly down,
I would tear from my forehead its beautiful crown,
To nestle once more in that haven of rest—
Your lips upon mine, my head on your breast.

You kissed me! My soul in a bliss so divine
Reeled and swooned like a drunkard when foolish with wine,
And I thought 'twere delicious to die there, if death
Would but come while my lips were yet moist with your breath;
While your arms clasped me round in that blissful embrace,
While your eyes melt in mine could e'en death e'er efface—
Oh, these are the questions I ask day and night:
Must my lips taste no more such exquisite delight?
Would you wish that your breast were my shelter as then?
And if you were here, would you kiss me again?

Josephine Slocum Hunt

KISSING

Come hither, womankind and all their worth,
Give me thy kisses as I call them forth.
Give me the billing kiss, that of the dove,
   A kiss of love;
The melting kiss, a kiss that doth consume
   To a perfume;
The extract kiss, of every sweet a part
   A kiss of art;
The kiss which ever stirs some new delight,
   A kiss of might;
The twactching smacking kiss, and where you cease,
   A kiss of peace;
The music kiss, and-quaver time;
   The kiss of rhyme;
The kiss of eloquence, which doth belong
   Unto the tongue;
The kiss of all the sciences in one,
   The Kiss alone.
So, 'tis enough.

Lord Herbert of Cherbury

NO AND YES

If I could choose my paradise,
   And please myself with choice of bliss,
Then I would have your soft blue eyes
   And rosy little mouth to kiss!
Your lips, as smooth and tender, child,
As rose-leaves in a coppice wild.

If fate bade choose some sweet unrest,
   To weave my troubled life a snare,
Then I would say "her maiden breast
   And Golden ripple of her hair";
And weep amid those tresses, child,
Contented to be thus beguiled.

Thomas Ashe

LOVE'S PHILOSOPHY

The fountains mingle with the river,
   And the rivers with the ocean,
The winds of heaven mix forever
   With a sweet emotion;
Nothing in the world is single;
   All things by a law divine
In one another's being mingle;—
   Why not I with thine?

See the mountains kiss high heaven,
   And the waves clasp one another;
No sister flower would be forgiven
   If it disdained its brother;
And the sunlight clasps the earth,
   And the moonbeams kiss the sea;
What are all these kissings worth,
   If thou kiss not me?

Percy Bysshe Shelley

Trust and Doubt
※※

YOUNG LOVE

Within my bed, the whole night thru,
I turn and turn . . . and think of you;
And wonder, when we met to-day,
If you said what you meant to say.
And what you thought I thought you meant
And were you sorry when I went;
And did you get my meaning when . . .
And then the whole thing through again!
I only hope that somewhere you
Are sleeping badly too!

Theodosia Garrison

DID NOT

'Twas a new feeling—something more
Than we had dared to own before,
  Which then we hid not;
We saw it in each other's eye,
And wished, in every half-breathed sigh,
  To speak, but did not.

She felt my lips' impassioned touch—
'Twas the first time I dared so much,
  And yet she chid not;
But whispered o'er my burning brow,
'Oh, do you doubt I love you now?'
  Sweet soul! I did not.

Warmly I felt her bosom thrill,
I pressed it closer, closer still,
  Though gently bid not;
Till—oh! the world hath seldom heard
Of lovers, who so nearly erred,
And yet, who did not.

Thomas Moore

UNTITLED
***

Maid, will ye love me, yea or no?
Tell me the truth, and let me go.
It can be no less tha a sinful deed,
    Trust me truly,
To linger a lover that looks to speed
    In due time duly.

You maids, that think yourselves as fine
As Venus and all the Muses nine,
The Father himself, and He first made Man,
    Trust me truly,
Made you for his help, when the world began,
    In due time duly.

The sith God's will was even so
Why should you disdain your lover tho?
But rather with a willing heart
    Love him truly:
For in so doing you do but your part;
    Let reason rule ye.

Consider, sweet, what sighs and sobs
Do nip my heart with cruel throbs
And all, my dear, for love of you,
    Trust me truly;
But I hope that you will some mercy show
    In due time duly.

Anonymous

LOVE ME AT LAST
*****

Love me at last, or if you will not,
    Leave me;
Hard words could never, as these half-words,
    Grieve me:
Love me at last—or leave me.

Love me at last, or let the last word uttered
    Be but your own;
Love me, or leave me—as a cloud, a vapor,
    Or a bird flown.
Love me at last—I am but sliding water
    Over a stone.

Alice Corbin

INTIMATES

Don't you care for my love? she said bitterly.

I handed her the mirror, and said:
Please address these questions to the proper person!
Please make all requests to head-quarters!
In all matters of emotional importance
   please approach the supreme authority direct!—
So I handed her the mirror.

D. H. Lawrence

SO BEAUTIFUL YOU ARE INDEED

So beautiful you are, indeed,
That I am troubled when you come,
And though I crave you for my need,
Your nearness strikes me blind and dumb.

And when you bring your lips to mine
My spirit trembles and escapes,
And you and I are turned divine,
Bereft of our familiar shapes.

And fearfully we tread cold space,
Naked of flesh and winged with flame,
. . . Until we find us face to face,
Each calling on the other's name!

Irene Rutherford McLeod

MENACE

I came into your room and spoke.
   Sudden I knew you were not there.
The easy, common sentence broke
   Against the unanswering air.

My heart shook like a frightened bird,
   And to my ear the terror said,
Where nothing spoke and nothing stirred,—
   Dear God, if he were dead!

I heard your footstep in the house,
   Your voice brought comfort to my fear.
But, fluttering like a frightened mouse,
   My heart beat at my ear.

The room wore its familiar face;
   On the warm hearth spirited the flame
Yet—menace of an empty place—
   Lord, if he never came!

Katharine Tynan

UNTITLED
***

Ah, Love! let us be true
To one another; for the world, which seems
To lie before us like a land of dreams,
So various, so beautiful, so new,
Hath really neither joy, nor love, nor light,
Nor certitude, nor peace, nor help for pain;
And we are here as on a darkling plain,
Swept with confused alarms of struggle and flight
Where ignorant armies clash by night.

Matthew Arnold

UNTITLED
**

Tell me dearest, what is love
'Tis a lightning from above;
'Tis an arrow, 'tis a fire
'Tis a boy they call Desire.
   'Tis a grave
   Gapes to have
Those poor fools that long to prove.

Tell me more, are women true?
Yes, some are, and some as you.
Some are willing, some are strange,
Since you men first taught to change.
   And till troth
   Be in both,
All shall love, to love anew.

Tell me more yet, can they grieve?
Yes, and sicken sore, but live,
And be wise, and delay,
When you men are wise as they.
   Then I see
   Faith will be,
Never till they both believe.

J. Fletcher

FULLNESS OF LOVE

If I leave all for thee, wilt thou exchange
And *be* all to me? Shall I never miss
Home-talk and blessing, and the common kiss
That comes to each in turn, nor count it strange,
When I look up, to drop on a new range
Of walls and floors, . . . another home than this?
Nay, wilt thou fill that place by me which is
Filled by dead eyes too tender to know change?
That's hardest! If to conquer love, has tried,
To conquer grief tries more . . . as all things prove,
For grief indeed is love and grief beside.
Alas, I have grieved so I am hard to love—
Yet love me—wilt thou? Open thine heart wide,
And fold within the wet wings of thy love.

Elizabeth Barrett Browning

DEBTS

My debt to you, Belovèd,
   Is one I cannot pay
In any coin of any realm
   On any reckoning day;

For where is he shall figure
   The debt, when all is said,
To one who makes you dream again
   When all the dreams were dead?

Or where is the appraiser
   Who shall the claim compute
Of one who makes you sing again
   When all the songs were mute?

Jessie B. Rittenhouse

WHY SO PALE AND WAN

Why so pale and wan, fond lover?
 Prithee why so pale?
Will, when looking well can't move her,
 Looking ill prevail?
 Prithee why so pale?

Why so dull and mute, young sinner?
 Prithee why so mute?
Will, when speaking well can't win her,
 Saying nothing do't?
 Prithee why so mute?

Quit, quit for shame; this will not move,
 This cannot take her;
If of herself she will not love,
 Nothing can make her;
 The devil take her!

John Suckling

DO YOU REMEMBER

Do you remember when you heard
My lips breath love's first faltering word?
   You do, sweet—don't you?
When, having wandered all the day,
Linked arm in arm I dared to say,
   "You'll love me—won't you?"

And when you blushed, and could not speak,
I fondly kissed your glowing cheek;
   Did that affront you?
Oh, surely not; your eye exprest
No wrath, but said, perhaps in jest,
   "You'll love me—won't you?"

I'm sure my eyes replied, "I will."
And you believe that promise still;
   You do, sweet—don't you?
Yes, yes, when age has made our eyes
Unfit for questions or replies,
   You'll love me—won't you?

Thomas Haynes Bayly

KISS ME SOFTLY

Kiss me softly and speak to me low,—
   Malice has ever a vigilant ear;
   What if malice were lurking near?
     Kiss me, dear!
Kiss me softly and speak to me low.

Kiss me softly and speak to me low,—
   Envy too has watchful ear;
   What if envy should chance to hear?
     Kiss me, dear!
Kiss me softly and speak to me low.

Kiss me softly and speak to me low,—
   Trust me, darling, the time is near
   When lovers may love with never a fear,—
     Kiss me, dear!
Kiss me softly and speak to me low.

John Godfrey Saxe

UNTITLED
***

    Take, O take, those lips away,
        That sweetly were forsworn;
And those eyes, the break of day,
        Lights that do mislead the morn:
But my kisses bring again
Bring again:
Seals of love but sealed in vain,
—sealed in vain!

                William Shakespeare

UNTITLED

Prithee, Cloe, not so fast:
Let's not run and wed in haste;
We've a thousand things to do;
You must fly and I pursue,
You must frown, and I must sigh,
I entreat, and you deny.
Stay—If I am never crossed,
Half the pleasure will be lost;
Be, or seem to be, severe;
Give me the reason to despair;
Fondness will my wishes cloy,
Make me careless of the joy.
Lovers may, of course, complain
Of their troubles and their pain;
But, if their pain and trouble cease,
Love without it will not please.

John Oldmixon

FIDELIS
**

You have taken back the promise
   That you spoke so long ago;
Taken back the heart you gave me—
   I must even let it go.
Where Love once has breathed, Pride dieth;
   So I struggled, but in vain,
First to keep the links together,
   Then to piece the broken chain.

But it might not be—so freely
   All your friendship I restore,
And the heart that I had taken
   As my own forevermore.
No shade of reproach shall touch you,
   Dread no more a claim from me—
But I will not have you fancy
   That I count myself as free.

I am bound by the old promise;
   What can break that golden chain?
Not even the words that you have spoken,
   Or the sharpness of my pain:
Do you think, because you fail me
And draw back your hand today,
That from out the heart I gave you
   My strong love can fade away?

It will live. No eyes may see it;
   In my soul it will lie deep,
Hidden from all; but I shall feel it
   Often stirring in its sleep.
So remember that the friendship
   Which you now think poor and vain,

Will endure in hope and patience,
　　Till you ask for it again.

Perhaps in some long twilight hour,
　　Like those we have known of old,
When past shadows gather round you,
　　And your present friends grow cold,
You may stretch your hands out towards me—
Ah! You will—I know not when—
I shall nurse my love and keep it
　　Faithfully, for you, till then.

Adelaide Anne Procter

SWEET PERIL

Alas, how easily things go wrong!
A sigh too much, or a kiss too long,
And there follows a mist and a weeping rain,
And life is never the same again.

Alas, how hardly things go right!
'Tis hard to watch in a summer night,
For the sigh will come, and the kiss will stay,
And the summer night is a wintry day.

And yet how easily things go right,
If the sigh and a kiss of a summer's night
Come deep from the soul in the stronger ray
That is born in the light of the winter's day.

And things can never go badly wrong
If the heart be true and the love be strong,
For the mist if it comes, and the weeping rain
Will be changed by the love into the sunshine again.

George MacDonald

SERENADE

By day my timid passions stand
   Like begging children at your gate,
Each with a mute, appealing hand
   To ask a dole of Fate;
But when night comes, released from doubt,
   Like merry minstrels they appear,
The stars ring out their hopeful shout,
   Beloved, can you hear?

They dare not sing to you by day
   Their all-desirous song, or take
The world with their adventurous lay
   For your enchanted sake.
But when the night-wind wakes and thrills
   The shadows that the night unbars,
Their music fills the dreamy hills,
   And folds the friendly stars.

Beloved, can you hear? They sing
   Words that no mortal lips can sound;
Love through the world has taken wing,
   My passions are unbound.
And now, and now, my lips, my eyes,
   Are stricken dumb with hope and fear,
It is my burning soul that cries,
   Beloved, can you hear?

Richard Middleton

CHILD, CHILD

Child, child, love while you can
The voice and the eyes and the soul of a man,
Never fear though it break your heart—
Out of the wound new joy will start;
Only love proudly and gladly and well
Though love be heaven or love be hell.

Child, child, love while you may,
For life is short as a happy day;
Never fear the thing you feel—
Only by love is life made real;
Love, for the deadly sins are seven,
Only through love will you enter heaven.

Sara Teasdale

UNTITLED
***

I prithee send me back my heart,
   Since I cannot have thine:
For if from yours you will not part,
   When then shouldst thou have mine?

Yet now I think on't, let it lie:
   To find it were in vain,
For thou hast a thief in either eye
   Would steal it back again.

Why should two hearts in one breast lie,
   And yet not lodge together?
O love, where is thy sympathy,
   If thus our breasts thou sever?

But love is such a mystery,
   I cannot find it out:
For when I think I'm best resolved,
   I then am in most doubt.

The farewell care, and farewell woe,
   I will no longer pine:
For I believe I have her heart
   As much as she has mine.

Attributed to Henry Hughes
and Sir John Suckling

UNTITLED
※

I looked and saw your eyes in the shadow of your hair,
As a traveler sees the stream in the shadow of the wood,
And I said, "My faint heart sighs, ah me! to linger there,
To drink deep and to dream in that sweet solitude."

I looked and saw your heart in the shadow of your eyes,
As a seeker sees the gold in the shadow of the stream,
And I said, "Ah, me! what art should win the immortal prize,
Whose want must make life cold and Heaven a hollow dream?"

I looked and saw your love in the shadow of your heart,
As a diver sees the pearl in the shadow of the sea;
And I murmured, not above my breath, but all apart,—
"Ah! you can love, true girl, and is your love for me?"

Dante Gabriel Rossetti

SONG

When I am dead, my dearest,
   Sing no sad songs for me;
Plant thou no roses at my head,
   Nor shady cypress-tree:
Be the green grass above me
   With showers and dewdrops wet;
And if thou wilt, remember,
   And if thou wilt, forget.

I shall not see the shadows,
   I shall not feel the rain;
I shall not hear the nightingale
   Sing on, as if in pain:
And dreaming through the twilight
   That doth not rise nor set,
Haply I may remember
   And haply may forget.

Christina Georgina Rossetti

LOVE NOT ME FOR COMELY GRACE

Love not me for comely grace,
For my pleasing eye or face;
Nor for any outward part,
No, nor for a constant heart:
   For these may fail or turn to ill,
     So thou and I shall sever.
Keep, therefore, a true woman's eye,
And love me still, but know not why;
   So hast thou the same reason still
     To doat upon me ever.

Anonymous

TO A LADY ASKING HIM
HOW LONG HE WOULD LOVE HER

It is not, Celia, in our power
   To say how long our love will last;
It may be we within this hour
   May lose those joys we now do taste:
The Blessed, that immortal be,
From change in love are only free.

Then since we mortal lovers are,
   Ask not how long our love will last;
But while it does, let us take care
   Each minute be with pleasure passed:
Were it not madness to deny
To live because we're sure to die?

George Etherege

Separation

***

THE WANT OF YOU

The want of you is like no other thing;
It smites my soul with sudden sickening;
It binds my being with a wreath of rue—
   This want of you.

It flashes on me with the waking sun;
It creeps upon me when the day is done;
It hammers at my heart the long night through—
   This want of you.

It sighs within me with the misting skies;
Oh, all the day within my heart it cries,
Old as your absence, yet each moment new—
   This want of you.

Mad with demand and aching with despair,
It leaps within my heart and you are—where?
God has forgotten, or he never knew—
   This want of you.

Ivan Leonard Wright

THE HAUNTED HEART

I am not wholly yours, for I can face
   A world without you in the years to be,
   And think of love that has been given me
By other men, and wear it as a grace;
Yes, even in your arms there is a space
   That yet might widen to infinity,
   And deep within your eyes I still can see
Old memories that I cannot erase.

But let these ghostly tenants of the heart
    Stay on unchallenged through changing days
    And keep their shadowy leaseholds without fear,
Then if the hour should come when we must part,
We know that we shall go on haunted ways,
    Each to the end inalienably dear.

Jessie B. Rittenhouse

WHEN I AM NOT WITH YOU

When I am not with you
I am alone,
For there is no one else
And there is nothing
That comforts me but you.
When you are gone
Suddenly I am sick,
Blackness is round me,
There is nothing left.
I have tried many things,
Music and cities,
Stars in their constellations
And the sea,
But there is nothing
That comforts me but you;
And my poor pride bows down
Like grass in a rain storm
Drenched with my longing
The night is unbearable,
Oh, let me go to you
For there is no one,
There is nothing
To comfort me but you.

Sara Teasdale

TWO LIPS

I kissed them in fancy as I came
   Away in the morning glow:
I kissed them through the glass of her picture-frame:
   She did not know.

I kissed them in love, in troth, in laughter,
   When she knew all; long so!
That I should kiss them in a shroud thereafter
   She did not know.

Thomas Hardy

THE ANSWERING VOICE
*
**

How strange I once denied him
   What took so little while.
A kiss would seem so simple
   So slight a thing a smile.

With pleased sweet looks of wonder
   He took what I could give,—
Such words as we deny them
   Only because they live.

The pale light of the morning
   Shone in upon the wall.
Come back to me, my darling,
   And I will give you all.

Anna Hempstead Branch

BHARTRHARI

In former days we'd both agree
That you were me, and I was you.
What has now happened to us two,
That you are you, and I am me?

*Translated from the
Sanskrit by John Brough*

FORGIVEN

I dreamed so dear a dream of you last night!
I thought you came. I was so glad, so gay,
I whispered, "Those were foolish words to say;
I meant them not. I cannot bear the sight
Of your dear face. I cannot meet the light
Of your dear eyes upon me. Sit, I pray,—
Sit here beside me; turn your look away,
And lay your cheek on mine." Till morning bright
We sat so, and we did not speak. I knew
All was forgiven; so I nestled there
With your arms round. Swift the sweet hours flew.
At last I waked, and sought you everywhere.
How long, dear, think you, that my glad cheek will
Burn,—as it burns with your cheek's pressure still?

Helen Hunt Jackson

UNTITLED
***

it may not always be so; and i say
that if your lips, which i have loved, should touch
another's, and your dear strong fingers clutch
his heart, as mine in time not far away;
if on another's face your sweet hair lay
in such a silence as i know, or such
great writhing words as, uttering overmuch,
stand helplessly before the spirit at bay;

if this should be, i say if this should be—
you of my heart, send me a little word;
that i may go unto him, and take his hands,
saying, Accept all happiness from me.
Then shall i turn my face, and hear one bird
sing terribly afar in the lost islands.

e. e. cummings

POSTSCRIPT: FOR GWENO

If I should go away,
Beloved, do not say
'He has forgotten me.'
For you abide,
A singing rib within my dreaming side;
You always stay.
And in the mad tormented valley
Where blood and hunger rally
And Death the wild beast is uncaught, untamed,
Our soul withstands the terror
And has its quiet honour
Among the glittering stars your voices named.

Alun Lewis

SONG: HOW CAN I CARE?

How can I care whether you sigh for me
   While still I sleep alone swallowing back
The spittle of desire, unmanned, a tree
    Pollarded of its crown, a dusty sack
    Tossed on the stable rack?

How can I care what coloured frocks you wear,
   What humming-birds you watch on jungle hills,
What phosphorescence wavers in your hair,
    Or with what water-music the night fills—
    Dear love, how can I care?

Robert Graves

FOUND

Oh, when I saw your eyes,
So old it was, so new, the hushed surprise:
After a long, long search, it came to be,
    Home folded me.

And looking up, I saw
The far, first stars like tapers to my awe,
In the dim hands of hid, benignant Powers,
    At search long hours.

And did they hear us call,
That they have found us children after all?
And did you know, O Wonderful and Dear,
    That I was here?

Josephine Preston Peabody

WHEN WE ARE PARTED

When we are parted let me lie
  In some far corner of thy heart,
  Silent, and from the world apart,
Like a forgotten melody:
Forgotten of the world beside,
  Cherished by one, and one alone,
  For some loved memory of its own;
So let me in thy heart abide
    When we are parted.

When we are parted, keep for me
  The sacred stillness of the night;
  That hour, sweet Love, is mine by right;
Let others claim the day of thee!
The cold world sleeping at our feet,
  My spirit shall discourse with thine;—
  When stars upon thy pillow shine,
At thy heart's door I stand and beat,
    Though we are parted.

Hamilton Aidé

I SOUGHT YOU
**

I sought you but I could not find you, all night long
   I called you, but you would not answer—all the night
     I wandered over hill and valley; heaven was bright
With crowded stars, and I was calling you in many a song.

The road through wood and meadow rambled here and there:
   Few were the travellers on that lonely road, and none
     Had heard of you, by wood or meadowland—not one
Had heard of you, or seen you passing anywhere.

At midnight, thirsting for your loveliness, I lay
   Under the shadow of the leafy hill, and cried
     Three times, calling upon your name. No voice replied . . .
The pebbly brooks went babbling, babbling, all the way.

The waters had a drowsy sound, the hills were steep—
   My heart grew tired travelling; but there was no place
     That suited me and I was homesick for your face.
Dreaming of you, at the wood's edge I fell asleep.

John Hall Wheelock

PARTING

Dear Love, it was so hard to say
   Good-bye to-day!
You turned to go, yet going turned to stay!
Till suddenly at last you went away.

Then all at last I found my love unsaid,
   And bowed my head;
And went in tears up to my lonely bed—
Oh, would it be like this if you were dead?

Alice Freeman Palmer

THE TAXI

When I go away from you
The world beats dead
Like a slackened drum.
I call out for you against the jutted stars
And shout into the ridges of the wind.
Streets coming fast,
One after the other,
Wedge you away from me,
And the lamps of the city prick my eyes
So that I can no longer see your face.
Why should I leave you,
To wound myself upon the sharp edges of the night?

Amy Lowell

TO MARY: I SLEEP WITH THEE, AND WAKE WITH THEE

I sleep with thee, and wake with thee,
    And yet thou art not there;
I fill my arms with thoughts of thee,
    And press the common air.
Thy eyes are gazing upon mine,
    When thou art out of sight;
My lips are always touching thine,
    At morning, noon, and night.

I think and speak of other things
    To keep my mind at rest:
But still to thee my memory clings
    Like love in woman's breast.
I hide it from the world's wide eye,
    And think and speak contrary;
But soft the wind comes from the sky,
    And whispers tales of Mary.

The night wind whispers in my ear,
    The moon shines in my face;
A burden still of chilling fear
    I find in every place.
The breeze is whispering in the bush,
    And the dews fall from the tree,
All sighing on, and will not hush,
    Some pleasant tales of thee.

John Clare

UNTITLED

Stay, O sweet, and do not rise,
The light that shines comes from thine eyes;
The day breaks not, it is my heart,
Because that you and I must part.
   Stay, or else my joys will die,
   And perish in their infancy.

Anonymous

A SONG

Absent from thee, I languish still;
   Then ask me not, when I return?
The straying fool 'twill plainly kill
   To wish all day, all night to mourn.

Dear! from thine arms then let me fly,
   That my fantastic mind may prove
The torments it deserves to try
   That tears my fixed heart from my love.

When, wearied with a world of woe,
   To thy safe bosom I retire
Where love and peace and truth does flow,
   May I contented there expire,

Lest, once more wandering from that heaven,
   I fall on some base heart unblessed,
Faithless to thee, false, unforgiven,
   And lose my everlasting rest.

John Wilmot

GIFTS

You ask me what—since we must part—
   You shall bring back to me.
Bring back a pure and faithful heart
   As true as mine to thee.

You talk of gems from foreign lands,
   Of treasure, spoil, and prize.
Ah, love! I shall not search your hands
   But look into your eyes.

Juliana Horatia Ewing

THAT DAY YOU CAME

Such special sweetness was about
   That day God sent you here,
I knew the lavender was out,
   And it was mid of year.

Their common way the great winds blew,
   The ships sailed out to sea;
Yet ere that day was spent I knew
   Mine own had come to me.

As after song some snatch of tune
   Lurks still in grass or bough,
So, somewhat of the end o' June
   Lurks in each weather now.

The younger year sets the buds stir,
   The old year strips the trees;
But ever in my lavender
   I hear the brawling bees.

Lizette Woodworth Reese

UNTITLED
**

Take, O take those lips away,
   That so sweetly were forsworn,
And those eyes: the break of day
   Lights that do mislead the morn;
But my kisses bring again, bring again,
Seals of love, but seal'd in vain, seal'd in vain.

William Shakespeare

UNTITLED
***

Shall I come, sweet love, to thee
   When the evening beams are set?
Shall I not excluded be?
   Will you find no feignèd let?
Let me not, for pity, more
Tell the long hours at your door.

Who can tell what thief or foe,
   In the covert of the night,
For his prey will work my woe,
   Or through wicked foul despite?
So may I die unredrest
Ere my long love be possest.

But to let such dangers pass,
   Which a lover's thoughts disdain,
'Tis enough in such a place
   To attend love's joys in vain:
Do not mock me in thy bed,
While these cold nights freeze me dead.

Thomas Campion

TELEPATHY

"And how could you dream of meeting?"
   Nay, how can you ask me, sweet?
All day my pulse had been beating
   The tune of your coming feet.

And as nearer and ever nearer
   I felt the throb of your tread,
To be in the world grew dearer,
   And my blood ran rosier red.

Love called, and I could not linger,
   But sought the forbidden tryst,
As music follows the finger
   Of the dreaming lutanist.

And though you had said it and said it,
   "We must not be happy to-day,"
Was I not wiser to credit
   The fire in my feet than your nay?

James Russell Lowell

UNTITLED
***

You would have understood me, had you waited;
   I could have loved you, dear! as well as he:
Had we not been impatient, dear! and fated
    Always to disagree.

What is the use of speech? Silence were fitter:
   Lest we should still be wishing things unsaid.
Though all the words we ever spake were bitter,
    Shall I reproach you dead?

Nay, let this earth, your portion, likewise cover
    All the old anger, setting us apart:
Always, in all, in truth was I your lover;
    Always, I held your heart.

I have met other women who were tender,
    As you were cold, dear! with a grace as rare.
Think you, I turned to them, or made surrender,
    I who had found you fair?

Had we been patient, dear! ah, had you waited,
    I had fought death for you, better than he:
But from the very first, dear! we were fated
    Always to disagree.

Late, late, I come to you, now death discloses
    Love that in life was not to be our part:

On your low lying mound between the roses,
   Sadly I cast my heart.

I would not waken you; nay! this is fitter;
   Death and the darkness give you unto me;
Here we who loved so, were so cold and bitter,
   Hardly can disagree.

Paul Verlaine

AT THE CHURCH GATE

Although I enter not,
Yet round about the spot
   Ofttimes I hover:
And near the sacred gate,
With longing eyes I wait,
   Expectant of her.

The Minster bell tolls out
Above the city's rout
   And noise and humming
They've hushed the Minster bell:
The organ 'gins to swell:
   She's coming, she's coming!

My lady comes at last,
Timid, and stepping fast,
   And hastening hither,
With modest eyes downcast:
She comes—she's here—she's past—
   May Heaven go with her!

Kneel, undisturb'd, fair Saint!
Pour out your praise or plaint
   Meekly and duly;
I will not enter there,
To sully your pure prayer
   With thoughts unruly.

But suffer me to pace
Round the forbidden place,
　Lingering a minute,
Like outcast spirits who wait
And see through heaven's gate
　Angels within it.

William M. Thackeray

UNTITLED
***

When, dearest, I but think of thee,
Methinks all things that lovely be
   Are present and my soul delighted:
For beauties that from worth arise
Are like the grace of deities,
   Still present with us, tho' unsighted.

Thus while I sit and sigh the day
With all his borrowed lights away,
   Till night's black wings do overtake me,
Thinking on thee, thy beauties then,
As sudden lights do sleepy men,
   So they by their bright rays awake me.

Thus absence dies, and dying proves
No absence can subsist with loves
   That do partake of fair perfection:
Since in the darkest night they may
By love's quick motion find a way
   To see each other by reflection.

The waving sea can with each flood
Bathe some high promont that hath stood
   Far from the main up in the river:
O think not then but love can do
As much! for that's an ocean too,
Which flows not every day, but ever!

John Suckling

THE WIFE TO HER HUSBAND

Linger not long. Home is not home without thee:
  In dearest tokens do but make me mourn.
O, let its memory, like a chain about thee,
  Gently compel and hasten thy return!

Linger not long. Though crowds should woo thy staying,
  Bethink thee, can the mirth of thy friend, though dear,
Compensate for the grief thy long delaying
  Costs the fond heart that signs to have thee here?

Linger not long. How shall I watch thy coming,
  As evening shadows stetch o'er moor and dell;
When the wild bee hath ceased her busy humming,
  And silence hangs on all things like a spell!

How shall I watch for thee, when fears grow stronger,
  As night grows dark and darker on the hill!
How shall I weep, when I can watch no longer!
  Ah! art thou absent, art thou absent still?

Yet I shall grieve not, though the eye that seeth me
  Gazeth through tears that make its splendor dull;
For oh! I sometimes fear when thou art with me,
  My cup of happiness is all too full.

Haste, haste thee home unto thy mountain dwelling,
  Haste, as a bird unto its peaceful nest!
Haste, as a skiff, through tempests wide and swelling,
  Flies to its haven of securest rest!

Anonymous

APOLOGY
**

Be not angry with me that I bear
   Your colors everywhere,
  All through each crowded street,
    And meet
  The wonder-light in every eye,
    As I go by.

Each plodding wayfarer looks up to gaze,
   Blinded by rainbow haze,
  The stuff of happiness,
    No less,
  Which wraps me in its glad-hued folds
    Of peacock golds.

Before my feet the dusty, rough-paved way
   Flushes beneath its gray.
  My steps fall ringed with light,
    So bright,
  It seems a myriad suns are strown
    About the town.

Around me is the sound of steepled bells,
   And rich perfumèd smells
  Hand like a wind-forgotten cloud,
    And shroud
  Me from close contact with the world.
    I dwell impearled.

You blazon me with jeweled insignia.
  A flaming nebula
  Rims in my life. And yet
    You set
  The word upon me, unconfessed
    To go unguessed.

Amy Lowell

UNTITLED

I prithee send me back my heart,
    Since I can not have thine:
For if from yours you will not part,
    Why then shouldst thou have mine?

Yet now I think on't, let it lie:
    To find it were in vain,
For th' hast a thief in either eye
    Would steal it back again.

Why should two hearts in one breast lie,
    And yet not lodge together?
O love, where is thy sympathy,
    If thus our breasts thou sever?

But love is such a mystery,
    I cannot find it out:
For when I think I'm best resolved,
    I then am in most doubt.

Then farewell care, and farewell woe,
    I will no longer pine:
For I'll believe I have her heart
    As much as she has mine.

John Suckling

IF THOU WERT BY MY SIDE

If thou wert by my side, my love!
   How fast would evening fail
In green Bengala's palmy grove,
   Listening the nightingale!

If thou, my love! wert by my side,
   My babies at my knee,
How gayly would our pinnace glide
   O'er Gunga's mimic sea!

I miss thee at the dawning gray,
   When, on our deck reclined,
In careless ease my limbs I lay,
   And woo the cooler wind.

I miss thee when by Gunga's stream
   My twilight steps I guide,
But most beneath the lamp's pale beam,
   I miss thee from my side.

I spread my books, my pencil try,
   The lingering noon to cheer,
But miss thy kind, approving eye,
   Thy meek, attentive ear.

But when of morn and eve the star
   Beholds me on my knee,
I feel, though thou are distant far,
   Thy prayers ascend for me.

Then on! then on! where duty leads,
   My course be onward still,

O'er broad Hindostan's sultry meads,
   O'er black Almorah's hill.

That course, nor Delhi's kingly gates
   nor wild Malwah detain,
For sweet the bliss us both awaits
   By yonder western main.

Thy towers, Bombay, gleam bright, they say,
   Across the dark blue sea;
But ne'er were hearts so light and gay,
   As then shall meet in thee!

Reginald Heber

TO A LATE COMER

Why didst thou come into my life so late?
   If it were morning I could welcome thee
   With glad all-hails, and bid each hour to be
The willing servitor of thine estate,
Lading thy brave ships with Time's richest freight;
   If it were noonday I might hope to see
   On some fair height thy banners floating free,
And hear the acclaiming voices call thee great!
But it is nightfall and the stars are out;
   Far in the west the crescent moon hangs low,
     And near at hand the lurking shadows wait;
Darkness and silence gather round about,
   Lethe's black stream is near its overflow,—
     Ah, friend, dear friend, why didst thou come so late?

Julia C. R. Dorr

ONE

The world is naught till one is come
   Who is the world; then beauty wakes,
And voices sing that have been dumb.

The world is naught when one is gone
   Who was the world; then the heart breaks
That this is lost which once was won.

Dear love, this life, so passion-fraught,
   From you its bliss or sorrow takes;
With you is all; without you naught.

Arlo Bates

COME TO ME, DEAREST
*

Come to me, dearest, I'm lonely without thee,
Daytime and night-time, I'm thinking about thee;
Night-time and daytime, in dreams I behold thee;
Unwelcome the waking which cease to fold thee.
Come to me, darling, my sorrows to lighten,
Come in thy beauty to bless and to brighten;
Come in thy womanhood, meekly and lowly,
Come in thy lovingness, queenly and holy.

Swallows will flit round the desolate ruin,
Telling of spring and its joyous renewing;
And thoughts of thy love and its manifold treasure
Are circling my heart with a promise of pleasure.
O Spring of my spirit, O May of my bosom,
Shine out on my soul, till it bourgeon and blossom;
The waste of my life has a rose-root within it,
And thy fondness alone to the sunshine can win it.

Figure that moves like a song through the even;
Features lit up by a reflex of heaven;
Eyes like the skies of poor Erin, our mother,
Where shadow and sunshine are chasing each other;
Smiles coming seldom but childlike and simple,
Planting in each rosy cheek a sweet dimple;—
O, thanks to the Saviour that even thy seeming
Is left to the exile to brighten his dreaming.

You have been glad when you knew I was gladdened;
Dear, are you sad now to hear I am saddened?
Our hearts ever answer in tune and in time, love,
As octave to octave, and rhyme unto rhyme, love;
I cannot weep but your tears will be flowing,
You cannot smile but my cheek will be flowing;

I would not die without you at my side, love.
You will not linger when I shall have died, love.

Come to me, dear, ere I die of my sorrow,
Rise on my gloom like the sun of to-morrow;
Strong, swift, and fond as the words which I speak, love,
With a song on your lip, a smile on your cheek, love.
Come, for my heart in your absence is weary,—
Haste, for my spirit is sickened and dreary,—
Come to the arms which alone should caress thee,
Come to the heart that is throbbing to press thee!

Joseph Brenan

NO ONE SO MUCH AS YOU

No one so much as you
Love this my clay,
Or would lament as you
Its daying day.

You know me through and through
Though I have not told,
And though with what you know
You are not bold.

None ever was so fair
As I thought you:
Not a word can I bear
Spoken against you,

All that I ever did
For you seemed coarse
Compared with what I hid
Nor put in force.

My eyes scarce dare meet you
Lest they should prove
I but respond to you
And do not love.

We look and understand,
We cannot speak
Except in trifles and
Words the most weak.

For I at most accept
Your love, regretting

That is all: I have kept
Only a fretting

That I could not return
All that you gave
And could not ever burn
With the love you have,

Till sometimes it did seem
Better it were
Never to see you more
Than linger here

With only gratitude
Instead of love
A pine in solitude
Cradling a dove.

Edward Thomas

PARTING AFTER A QUARREL

You looked at me with eyes grown bright with pain,
   Like some trapped thing's. And then you moved your head
Slowly from side to side, as though the strain
   Ached in your throat with anger and with dread.

And then you turned and left me, and I stood
   With a queer sense of deadness over me,
And only wondered dully that you could
   Fasten your trench-coat up so carefully—

Till you were gone. Then all the air was quick
   With my last words, that seemed to leap and quiver;
And in my heart I heard the little click
   Of a door that closes—quietly, forever.

Eunice Tietjens

UNTITLED
***

Have I, this moment, led thee from the beach
Into the boat? now far beyond my reach!
Stand there a little while, and wave once more
That 'kerchief; but may none upon the shore
Dare think the fond salute was meant for him!
Dizzily on the splashing water swim
My heavy eyes, and sometimes can attain
Thy lovely form, which tears bear off again.
In vain have they now ceast; it now is gone
Too far for sight, and leaves me here alone.
O could I hear the creaking of the mast!
I curse it present, I regret it past.

Walter Savage Landor

IMAGES

I

Through the dark pine trunks
Silver and yellow gleam the clouds
And the sun;
The sea is faint purple.
My love, my love, I shall never reach you.

II

You are beautiful
As a straight red fox-glove
Among green plants;
I stretched out my hand to caress you:
It is blistered by the envious nettles.

III

I have spent hours this morning
Seeking in the brook
For a clear pebble
To remind me of your eyes.
And all the sleepless hours of night
I think of you.

IV

Your kisses are poignant,
Ah! why must I leave you?
Here alone I scribble and re-scribble
The words of a long-dead Greek poet:
"Love, thou art terrible,
Ah, Love, thou art bitter-sweet!"

Richard Aldington

YOU AND I

My hand is lonely for your clasping, dear;
   My ear is tired waiting for your call.
I want your strength to help, your laugh to cheer;
   Heart, soul and senses need you, one and all.
I droop without your full, frank sympathy;
   We ought to be together—you and I;
We want each other so, to comprehend
   The dream, the hope, things planned, or seen, or wrought.
Companion, comforter and guide and friend,
   As much as love asks love, does thought ask thought.
Life is so short, so fast the lone hours fly,
   We ought to be together, you and I.

Henry Alford

THE LOST MISTRESS

All's over, then: does truth sound bitter
   As one at first believes?
Hark, 'tis the sparrows' good-night twitter
   About your cottage eaves!

And the leaf-buds on the vine are wooly,
   I noticed that, to-day;
One day more bursts them open fully
   —You know the red turns grey.

To-morrow we meet the same then, dearest?
   May I take your hand in mine?
Mere friends are we,—well, friends the merest
   Keep much that I'll resign:

For each glance of that eye so bright and black,
   Though I keep with heart's endeavour,—
Your voice, when you wish the snowdrops back,
   Though it stay in my soul for ever!—

Yet I will but say what mere friends say,
   Or only a thought stronger;
I will hold your hand but as long as all may,
   Or so very little longer!

Robert Browning

UNTITLED
***

Ah! yesterday was dark and drear,
   My heart was deadly sore;
Without thy love it seemed, my Dear,
   That I could live no more.

And yet I laugh and sing to-day;
   Care or care not for me,
Thou canst not take the love away
   With which I worship thee.

And if to-morrow, Dear, I live,
   My heart I shall not break:
For still I hold it that to give
   Is sweeter than to take.

Mathilde Blind

REMEMBER

Remember me when I am gone away,
   Gone far away into the silent land;
   When you can no more hold me by the hand,
Nor I half turn to go, yet turning stay.
Remember me when no more day by day
   You tell me of our future that you planned:
   Only remember me; you understand
It will be late to counsel then or pray.
Yet if you should forget me for a while
   And afterwards remember, do not grieve:
   For if the darkness and corruption leave
   A vestige of thought that once I had,
Better by far you should forget and smile
   Than you should remember and be sad.

Christina Georgina Rossetti

OUR OWN

If I had known in the morning
   How wearily all the day
The words unkind would trouble my mind
That I said when you went away,
I had been more careful, darling,
   Nor given you needless pain;
But we vex our own with look and tone
We may never take back again.

For though in the quiet evening
   You may give me the kiss of peace,
Yet it well might be that never for me
   The pain of the heart should cease!
How many go forth in the morning
   Who never come home at night!
And hearts have broken for harsh words spoken
   That sorrow can ne'er set right.

We have careful thought for the stranger,
   And smiles for the sometime guest;
And oft for "our own" the bitter tone,
   Though we love our own the best.
Ah! lips with the curve impatient,
   Ah! brow with the shade of scorn,
'Twere a cruel fate, were the night too late
   To undo the work of the morn!

Margaret E. Sangster

SONG

A place in thy memory, dearest,
   Is all that I claim,
To pause and look back when thou hearest
The sound of my name.
Another may woo thy nearer,
Another may win and wear;
I care not, though he be dearer,
If I am remembered there.

Could I be thy true lover, dearest,
   Couldst thou smile on me,
I would be the fondest and nearest
   That ever loved thee.
But a cloud o'er my pathway is glooming
Which never must break upon thine,
And Heaven, which made thee all blooming,
Ne'er made thee to wither on mine.

Remember me not as a lover
   Whose fond hopes are crossed,
Whose bosom can never recover
   The light it has lost;
As the young bride remembers the mother
She loves, yet never may see,
As a sister remembers a brother,
Oh, dearest, remember me.

Gerald Griffin

UNTITLED
***

Oh, when I was in love with you,
   Then I was clean and brave,
And miles around the wonder grew
   How well did I behave.

And now the fancy passes by,
   And nothing will remain,
And miles around they'll say that I
   Am quite myself again.

A. E. Housman

THOU HAST WOUNDED
THE SPIRIT THAT LOVED THEE

Thou hast wounded the spirit that loved thee,
   And cherished thine image for years,
Thou has taught me at last to forget thee,
   In secret, in silence, and tears,
As a young bird when left by its mother,
   Its earliest pinions to try,
Round the nest will still lingering hover,
   Ere its trembling wings to try.

Thus we're taught in this cold world to smother
   Each feeling that once was so dear;
Like that young bird I'll seek to discover
   A home of affection elsewhere.
Though this heart may still cling to thee fondly
   And dream of sweet memories past,
Yet hope, like the rainbow of summer,
   Gives a promise of Lethe at last.

Like the sunbeams that play on the ocean,
   In tremulous touches of light,
Is the heart in its early emotion,
   Illumined with versions as bright.
Yet oftimes beneath the waves swelling,
   A tempest will suddenly come,
All rudely and wildly dispelling
   The love of the happiest home.

Mrs. David Porter

I'LL REMEMBER YOU, LOVE, IN MY PRAYERS

When the curtains of night are pinned back by the stars,
    And the beautiful moon leaps the skies,
And the dewdrops of heaven are kissing the rose,
    It is then that my memory flies
As if on the wings of some beautiful dove
    In haste with the message it bears
To bring you a kiss of affection and say:
    I'll remember you, love, in my prayers.

Go where you will, on land or on sea,
    I'll share all your sorrows and cares;
And at night, when I kneel by my bedside to pray
    I'll remember you, love, in my prayers.

I have loved you too fondly to ever forget
    The love you have spoken to me;
And the kiss of affection still warm on my lips
    When you told me how true you would be.
I know not if fortune be fickle or friend,
    Or if time on your memory wears;
I know that I love you wherever you roam,
    And remember you, love, in my prayers.

When angels in Heaven are guarding the good,
    As God has ordained them to do,
In answer to prayers I have offered Him,
    I know there is one watching you.
And may its bright spirit be with you through life
    To guide you up heaven's bright stairs,
And meet with the one who has loved you so true
    And remembered you, love, in her prayers.

Anonymous

NIGHT AND LOVE

When stars are in the quiet skies,
   Then most I pine for thee;
Bend on me, then, thy tender eyes,
   As stars look on the sea!

For thoughts, like waves that glide by night,
   Are stillest when they shine;
Mine earthly love lies hushed in light
   Beneath the heaven of thine.

There is an hour when angels keep
   Familiar watch o'er men,
When coarser souls are wrapped in sleep—
   Sweet spirit, meet me then.

There is an hour when holy dreams
   Through slumber fairest glide;
And in that mystic hour it seems
   Thou shouldst be by my side.

My thoughts of thee too sacred are
   For daylight's common beam:
I can but know thee as my star,
   My angel and my dream!

Edward George Earle Bulwer Lytton

STAR SONG

When sunset flows into golden glows
   And the breath of the night is new,
Love, find afar eve's eager star—
   That is my thought of you.

O tear-wet eye that scans the sky
   Your lonely lattice through:
Choose any one, from sun to sun—
   That is my thought of you.

And when you wake at the morning's break
   To rival rose and dew,
The star that stays till the leading rays—
   That is my thought of you.

Ay, though by day they seem away
   Beyond or cloud or blue,
From dawn to night unquenched their light—
   As are my thoughts of you.

Robert Underwood Johnson

MISS YOU

Miss you, miss you, miss you;
Everything I do
Echoes with the laughter
And the voice of You.
You're on every corner,
Every turn and twist,
Every old familiar spot
Whispers how you're missed.

Miss you, miss you, miss you!
Everywhere I go
There are poignant memories
Dancing in a row.
Silhouette and shadow
Of your form and face,
Substance and reality
Everywhere displace.

Oh, I miss you, miss you!
God! I miss you, Girl!
There's a strange, sad silence
'Mid the busy whirl,
Just as tho' the ordinary
Daily things I do
Wait with me, expectant
For a word from You.

Miss you, miss you, miss you!
Nothing now seems true
Only that 'twas heaven
Just to be with You.

David Cory

BELOVED, FROM THE HOUR THAT YOU WERE BORN
*
**

Beloved, from the hour that you were born
I loved you with the love whose birth is pain;
And now, that I have lost you, I must mourn
With mortal anguish, born of love again;
And so I know that Love and Pain are one,
Yet not one single joy would I forego.—
The very radiance of the tropic sun
Makes the dark night but darker here below.
Mine is no coward soul to count the cost;
The coin of love with lavish hand I spend,
And though the sunlight of my life is lost
And I must walk in shadow to the end,—
I gladly press the cross against my heart,
And welcome Pain, that is Love's counterpart!

Corinne Roosevelt Robinson

FAREWELL

Thou goest; to what distant place
   Wilt thou thy sunlight carry?
I stay with cold and clouded face:
   How long am I to tarry?
Where'er thou goest, morn will be;
Thou leavest night and gloom to me.

The night and gloom I can but take;
   I do not grudge thy splendor:
Bid souls of eager men awake;
   Be kind and bright and tender.
Give day to other worlds; for me
It must suffice to dream of thee.

John Addington Symonds

Acknowledgments

※※

The editors wish to acknowledge and thank the copyright holders for use of the following works:

"Man and Wife" from *Life Studies* by Robert Lowell, copyright © 1956, 1959 by Robert Lowell, reprinted by permission of Farrar, Straus and Giroux, Inc.

"Marriage" from *Honey Out of the Rock* by Babette Deutsch, reprinted by permission of Adam Yarmolinsky.

"A Song for My Mate" from *Bluestone* by Marguerite Wilkinson, copyright 1920 by Macmillan Publishing Co., renewed © 1948 by Natalie Bigelow, reprinted by permission of Macmillan Publishing Co.

"A Dedication to My Wife" from *Collected Poems 1900–1962* by T. S. Eliot, copyright 1936 by Harcourt Brace Jovanovich, Inc.; copyright © 1963, 1964 by T. S. Eliot. Reprinted by permission of Harcourt Brace Jovanovich, Inc., Farrar, Straus and Giroux, Inc., and Faber and Faber Ltd.

"A Decade" from *The Complete Poetical Works of Amy Lowell*, copyright 1955 by Houghton Mifflin Company, renewed © 1983 by Houghton Mifflin Company, Brinton P. Roberts, Esq. and G. D'Andelot Belin, Esq., reprinted by permission of Houghton Mifflin Company.

"The Heart of the Woman" by W. B. Yeats, from *The Poems of W. B. Yeats: A New Edition*, edited by Richard J. Finneran, published by Macmillan Publishing Co. and reprinted by permission of A. P. Watt Ltd. on behalf of Michael B. Yeats and Macmillan London Ltd.

"Calypso's Song to Ulysses" from *Ride the Nightmare* by Adrian Mitchell, reprinted by permission of Jonathan Cape Ltd.

"Love Song" by Harriet Monroe, reprinted by permission of Mrs. Marguerite F. Fetcher.

"Love Song" from *Collected Poems, Volume I: 1909–1939* by William Carlos Williams, reprinted by permission of New Directions Publishing Corp.

"Psalm to My Beloved" from *Body and Raiment* by Eunice Tietjens, copyright 1919 by Alfred A. Knopf, Inc., renewed © 1947 by Cloyd Head, reprinted by permission of Alfred A. Knopf, Inc.

"Intimates" from *The Complete Poems of D. H. Lawrence*, collected and edited by Vivian de Sola Pinto and F. Warren Roberts, copyright © 1964, 1971 by Angelo Ravagli and C. M. Weekley, Executors of the Estate of Frieda Lawrence Ravagli. Reprinted by permission of Viking Penguin Inc.

"The Haunted Heart" from *The Lifted Cup* by Jessie B. Rittenhouse, copyright 1921 by Jessie B. Rittenhouse, renewed © 1949 by The Florida Bank and Trust Company as Executor of the author and John C. Rittenhouse as Executor, reprinted by permission of Houghton Mifflin Company.

"When I Am Not With You" from *Collected Poems* by Sara Teasdale, copyright 1926 by Macmillan Publishing Co., renewed © 1954 by Mamie T. Wheless, reprinted by permission of Macmillan Publishing Co.

"Two Lips" from *Complete Poems* by Thomas Hardy, edited by James Gibson, copyright 1925 by Macmillan Publishing Co., renewed © 1953 by Lloyds Bank Ltd., reprinted by permission of Macmillan Publishing Co.

Untitled: "it may not always be so; and i say" from *Tulips and Chimneys* by E. E. Cummings, edited by George James Firmage, reprinted by permission of Liveright Publishing Corporation. Copyright © 1923, 1925, and renewed 1951, 1953 by E. E. Cummings. Copyright © 1973, 1976 by the Trustees for the E. E. Cummings Trust. Copyright © 1973, 1976 by George James Firmage.

"Song: How Can I Care?" from *Collected Poems 1975* by Robert Graves, copyright © 1975 by Robert Graves, reprinted by permission of Oxford University Press, Inc. and A. P. Watt Ltd., on behalf of the Executors of the Estate of Robert Graves.

"The Taxi" from *The Complete Poetical Works of Amy Lowell*, copyright 1955 by Houghton Mifflin Company, renewed © 1983 by Houghton Mifflin Company, Brinton P. Roberts, Esq. and G. D'Andelot Belin, Esq., reprinted by permission of Houghton Mifflin Company.

"Apology" from *The Complete Poetical Works of Amy Lowell*, copyright 1955 by Houghton Mifflin Company, renewed © 1983 by Houghton Mifflin Company, Brinton P. Roberts, Esq. and G. D'Andelot Belin, Esq., reprinted by permission of Houghton Mifflin Company.

"Parting After a Quarrel" from *Body and Raiment* by Eunice Tietjens, copyright 1919 by Alfred A. Knopf, Inc., renewed © 1947 by Cloyd Head, reprinted by permission of Alfred A. Knopf, Inc.

Untitled: "Oh, when I was in love with you" by A. E. Housman, copyright 1939, 1940, © 1965 by Holt, Rinehart and Winston, copyright © 1967, 1968 by Robert E. Symons, from *The Collected Poems of A. E. Housman*, reprinted by permission of Henry Holt and Co. Inc.

Every effort has been made to locate the copyright holders for works by the following authors, but without success:
Hamilton Aide, Richard Aldington, Walter Benton, Louise Bogan, James Branch Cabell, Major Calder Campbell, Alice Corbin, Frances Cornford, David Cory, Mary Carolyn Davies, Edwin Denby, Arthur Davison Ficke, Arthur L. Gillom, Josephine Slocum Hunt, Ludwig Lewisohn, Irene Rutherford McLeod, Marjorie Meeker, Robert Mezey, George Moore, Edwin Morgan, Grace Fallow Norton, Shaemas O'Sheel, Alice Freeman Palmer, Frederick Peterson, Mrs. David Porter, Kathleen Raine, Corinne Roosevelt Robinson, Leonora Speyer, Edward Thomas, Katharine Tynan, Helen Hay Whitney, John Hall Wheelock, Ivan Leonard Wright.